Differentiating Instruction With Menus

Physics

ADVANCED-LEVEL MENUS
Grades 9–12

Differentiating Instruction With Menus

Physics

Laurie E. Westphal, Ed.D.

PRUFROCK PRESS INC.
WACO, TEXAS

Prufrock Press Inc.
P.O. Box 8813
Waco, TX 76714-8813
Phone: (800) 998-2208
Fax: (800) 240-0333
http://www.prufrock.com

CONTENTS

PART I

All About Menus and Choice

Chapter 1

Choice

"For so many reasons, it is simply the right thing to do for this age group."

—Shared by a group of secondary teachers when asked why choice is important for their students

Why Is Choice Important?

Ask any adult if they would prefer to choose what to do or be told what to do, and of course, they are going to prefer the choice. Students, especially teenagers, have these same feelings. Although they may not always stand up and demand a choice if none are present, they benefit in many ways from having them.

One benefit of choice is its ability to meet the needs of so many different students and their varied learning preferences. The Dunedin College of Education (Keen, 2001) conducted a research study on the preferred learning styles of 250 gifted students. Students were asked to rank different learning options. Of the 13 different options described to the students, only one option did not receive at least one negative response, and that was choice. Although all students have different preferences, choice is the one option that meets all students' needs. Why? Well, it takes the focus from the teacher as the decision maker and allows students to decide what is best for them. What teenager would argue against being able to do something that they prefer to do? When given the opportunity to choose, students are going to choose what best fits their educational needs.

> *"I really was not sure how my students were going to react to these choices. I didn't want the menu to be viewed as busy work when we already had so much content to cover. I was surprised (and relieved) by how well they responded [to the choices]. Now, they want to have choice in everything, which is always up for negotiation."*
>
> —English II teacher

Another benefit of choice is its ability to address different learning preferences and ultimately offer the opportunity to better assess what students understand about the content being studied. During professional development, I often ask teachers what learning preferences are most addressed in the products they provide. Not surprisingly, visual and written products top the list. These two preferences are most popular for many reasons, including ease of grading, ease of organizing and managing, and lack of supplies needed. In looking back on all of the different products my students have created, however, I noticed that most often, the tactile, kinesthetic, and verbal products provided greater depth and complexity (Komarraju et al., 2011). After analyzing these "noisy" products, I have come to realize that if I really want to know what my students understand, I need to allow them to show me through their learning preference—and the most common preferences of my students are not visual-written. Most students prefer tactile-kinesthetic (Dunn & Honigsfeld, 2013; Ricca, 1984; Sagan, 2010; Snyder, 1999). Because these preferences are not always addressed during whole-class instruction, teachers need a strategy that can allow students to express themselves. Using choice to offer these opportunities can help address the needs of more students in our classrooms.

Another advantage of choice is a greater sense of independence for the students (Deci et al., 1991; Patall, 2013; Robinson et al., 2008). When teachers offer choice, students design and create a product based on what they envision, rather than what their teacher envisions. When students would enter my classroom, many times they had been trained by previous teachers to produce what the teacher wanted, not what the students thought would be best. Teaching my students that what they envision could be correct (and wonderful) could be a struggle. "Is this what you want?" or "Is this right?" were popular questions as we started the school year. As we progressed, and I continued to redirect their questions back to them ("Is that what you would like to show?" or "Does that seem right to you?"), students began to ask for my approval less; they became more independent in their work. They might still need assurance, but the phrasing was different, "This is what I have so far. Can I ask for help from Joe?" or "I don't like this; I am going to pick something else." When teachers allow students choice in the products they create to show their learning, the students can develop this independence.

Increased student focus and persistence is another benefit of offering choice. When students are making choices in the activities they wish to complete, they are more focused on the learning that is needed to create their choice products (Flowerday & Schraw, 2003; Ricca, 1984). Students become engaged when they learn information that can help them develop products that they are excited about creating. Many students struggle with the purpose of the information being taught in the classroom, and this can lead to behavior problems. Students may feel disconnected from the content and lose interest (Robinson et al., 2008). Instead, students will pay closer attention to instruction when an immediate application (the student's choice product) for the knowledge being presented in class is present. If students are excited about the product, they are more focused on the content; they are less likely to be off task during instruction.

Many a great educator has referred to the idea that the best learning takes place when the students have a desire to learn. Some students have a desire to learn anything that is new to them; others do not want to learn anything unless it has interest for them. By incorporating choice activities that require the students to stretch beyond what they already know, teachers create a void which needs to be filled. This void leads to a desire to learn.

A Point to Ponder: Making Good Choices Is a Skill

"I want my students to be independent, and it can be frustrating that they just can't make decisions for themselves. I hadn't thought I might need to actually teach decision-making skills."

—Secondary study skills teacher, after hearing me discuss choice as a skill

When we think of making a good choice as a skill, much like writing an effective paragraph or essay, it becomes easy enough to understand that we need to encourage students to make their own choices. In keeping with this analogy, students could certainly figure out how to write on their own, and perhaps even how to compose sentences and paragraphs, by modeling other examples. Imagine, however, the progress and strength of the writing produced when students are given guidance and even the most basic of instruction on how to accomplish the task. The written piece is still their own, but the quality of the finished piece is much stronger when guidance is given during the process. There is a reason why class time is spent in the AP classroom focusing on how to write an appropriate response to a document-based question (DBQ) or free-response question (FRQ). Students need to practice the skill before the big test in May. The same is true with choices; the quality of choices our high school students can make in the classroom is directly impacted by exposure and practice.

As with writing, students could make choices on their own, but when the teacher provides background knowledge and assistance, the choices become more meaningful and the products richer. All students certainly need guidance (even if our strong-willed high school students think they know it all), as the idea of choice may be new to them. Some students may only have experienced basic instructional choices, like choosing between two journal prompts or perhaps having the option of making either a poster or a PowerPoint presentation about the content being studied. Some may not have experienced even this level of choice. This lack of experience can cause frustration for both teacher and student.

Teaching Choices as a Skill

So, what is the best way to provide guidance and enable our students to develop the skill of making good choices while still allowing them to develop their individuality? First, choose the appropriate number of choices for your students. Although the goal might be to have students choose from 20 different options, teachers might start by having their students choose from three predetermined choices the first day (if they were using a game show menu, for instance, students might choose an activity from the first column). Then, after that product had been created, students could choose from another three options from another column a few days later, and perhaps from another three the following week. By breaking students' choices down, teachers reinforce how to approach or attack a more complex and/or varied choice format in the future. All students can work up to making complex choices from longer lists of options as their choice skill level increases.

Second, although our high school students feel they know everything now, they may still need guidance on how to select the option that is right for them. They may not automatically gravitate toward options without an exciting and detailed description of each choice. For the most part, students have been trained to produce what the teacher requests, which means that when given a choice, they may choose what seems to be the easiest and what the teacher most wants (then they can get to what they would prefer to be doing). This means that when the teacher discusses the different menu options, they must be equally as excited about each option. The discussion of the different choices must be somewhat animated and specific. For example, if the content is all very similar, the focus should be on the product: "If you want to create something you might see on YouTube, this one is for you!" or "If you want to be artistic, check this one as a maybe!" The more exposure students have to the processing the teacher provides, the more skillful they become in their choice making.

How Can Teachers Allow Choice?

"The GT students seem to get more involved in assignments when they have choice. They have so many creative ideas and the menus give them the opportunity to use them."

—Secondary social studies teacher, when asked about how students respond to having choices

When people visit a restaurant, they are all attending with the common goal of finding something on the menu to satisfy their hunger. We all hope that when students come into our classroom, they will have a hunger as well—a hunger for learning. Choice menus are a way of allowing students to choose how they would like to satisfy that hunger. At the very least, a menu is a list of choices that students use to choose an activity (or activities) they would like to complete to show their learning. At best, it is a complex system in which students are given point goals and complete different products to earn points (which are based on the levels of Bloom's revised taxonomy; Anderson & Krathwohl, 2001). These menus should have a way to incorporate a "free-choice" option for those picky eaters who would like to make a special order to satisfy their learning hunger.

The next few sections provide examples of different menu formats that will be used in this book. Each menu has benefits, limitations or drawbacks, and time considerations. An explanation of the free-choice option and its management will follow the information on each type of menu.

Tic-Tac-Toe Menu

"My students really enjoy the Tic-Tac-Toe menus, and I get them to stretch themselves without them realizing it."

— High school AP World Geography teacher

Description

The Tic-Tac-Toe menu (see Figure 1.1) is a well-known, commonly used menu that contains a total of eight predetermined choices and one free choice for students. These choices can range from task statements leading to product creation, complex and/or higher level processing questions, or leveled problems for solving. The choices can be created at the same level of Bloom's revised taxonomy or can be arranged in such a way to allow for the three different levels or objectives within a unit or topic. If all choices have been created at the same level of Bloom's revised taxonomy, then each choice carries the same weight for grading and has similar expectations for completion time and effort.

Benefits

Flexibility. This menu can cover either one topic in depth, three different topics, or three objectives within one content area. When this menu covers just one objective, and all tasks are from the same level of Bloom's revised taxonomy (preferably the highest), students have the option of completing three projects in a tic-tac-toe pattern, or simply picking three from the menu. When the menu covers three objectives, three different levels of Bloom's revised taxonomy, or three different learning preferences, students will need to complete a vertical or horizontal tic-tac-toe pattern only (either a vertical column or horizontal row) to be sure they have completed one activity from each objective, level, and learning style.

Figure 1.1. Tic-Tac-Toe menu example.

Stretching. When students make choices on this menu by completing a row or column based on its design, they will usually face one choice that is out of their comfort zone. This "stretch" may result from a task's level of Bloom's revised taxonomy, its product style, or its content. Students will complete this "uncomfortable" choice because they want to do the other two in that row or column.

Friendly design. Students quickly understand how to use this menu. It is nonthreatening because it does not contain points, and therefore it seems to encourage students to stretch out of their comfort zones.

Weighting. All products are equally weighted, so recording grades and maintaining paperwork are easily accomplished.

Short time period. They are intended for shorter periods of time, between 1–3 weeks based on the tasks found on the menu as well as the amount of class time allotted for students to work on the menu.

Limitations

Few topics. These menus only cover one or three topics.

Student compromise. Although this menu does allow choice, when following the guidelines of rows or columns only, the menu provides only six different ways to meet the goal. This restriction means a student will sometimes have to compromise and complete an activity they would not have chosen because it completes their tic-tac-toe. (This is not always bad, though!)

No "safety net." Because each product in this menu is recorded as its own grade, it is possible that a student could fail this menu. Other formats allow students to make a poor choice and still earn full credit by completing additional options.

Time Considerations

Tic-Tac-Toe menus usually are intended for shorter amounts of completion time—at the most, they could take up to 3 weeks with students working outside of class and submitting one product each week. If a menu focuses on one topic in-depth and the students have time in class to work on their products, the menu could be completed in one week.

Meal Menu

"Seemed pretty easy at first—after all it was only three things and I was thinking I would just have to draw a few equations. All the lunch and dinner real world stuff was hard— [I] had to really think."

—High school Algebra II student

Description

The Meal menu (see Figure 1.2) is a menu with a total of at least nine predetermined choices. The choices are created at the various levels of Bloom's revised taxonomy and incorporate different learning preferences, with the levels getting progressively higher and more complex as students progress from breakfast to lunch and then dinner. All products carry the same weight for grading and have similar expectations for completion time and effort.

Benefits

Great starter menu. This menu is very straightforward and easy to understand, so time is saved in presenting the completion expectations.

Flexibility. This menu can cover either one topic in depth or three different objectives or aspects within a topic, with each meal representing a different aspect. With this menu, students have the option of completing three products: one from each meal.

Chunkability. The Meal menu is very easy to break apart into smaller pieces. Whether you have students who need support in making choices or you only want to focus on one aspect of a topic at a time, this menu can accommodate these decisions. Students could be asked to select a breakfast while the rest of the menu is put on hold until the breakfast product is submitted, then a lunch product is selected, and so on.

Friendly design. Students quickly understand how to use this menu because of its real-world application.

Weighting. All products are equally weighted, so recording grades and maintaining paperwork are easily accomplished with this menu.

Short time period. Meal menus are intended for shorter periods of time, between 1–3 weeks.

Figure 1.2. Meal menu example.

Limitations

No "safety net." Because each product in this menu is recorded as its own grade, it is possible that a student could fail this menu, unless the teacher allows the optional dessert to replace a low grade on one of the meal products.

Time Considerations

Meal menus usually are intended for shorter amounts of completion time—at the most, they should take 3 weeks with students working outside of class and submitting one product each week. If the menu focuses on one topic in-depth and the students have time in class to work on their products, the menu could be completed in one week.

List Menu/"Challenge List"

"Of the different formats I tried this year, I really liked the challenge list format. I could modify the menu simply by changing the [point] goal. When I had a student test out of two days, I simply upped [their] goal to 140, and [they] worked on [their] menu during instructional time. It was a huge success!"

—Secondary math teacher

Description

The basic List menu (see Figure 1.3), or Challenge List, has a total of at least 10 predetermined choices, each with its own point value, and at least one free choice for students. Choices are simply listed with assigned points based on the levels of Bloom's revised taxonomy. The choices carry different weights and have different expectations for completion time and effort. A point criterion is set forth that equals 100%, and students choose how they wish to attain that point goal. There are different versions of the list menu included in this book: the Challenge List (one topic in depth) and a Multitopic List Menu (which, based on its structure, can accommodate more than one topic).

Benefits

Grade-as-you-go. This menu requires that teachers grade products as the students complete them. Actively grading and providing immediate feedback are important so the students can alter their plans and choose to submit additional products to be sure they reach the point goal. Additionally, by grading-as-you-go, teachers will not have piles of products to grade once the menu is completed.

Responsibility. Students have complete control over their grades. Students like the idea that they can guarantee their grade if they complete their required work and meet the expectations outlined in the rubric and product guidelines. If students do not earn full credit on one of the chosen products, they can complete another product to be sure they have met their point goal. This responsibility over their own grades also allows a shift in thinking about grades—whereas many students think of grades in terms of how the teacher judged their work, or what the teacher "gave me," having control over their grades leads students to understand that they earn their grades.

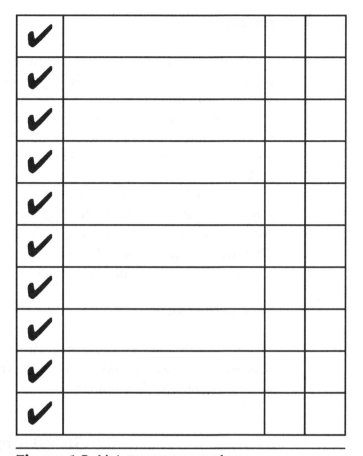

Figure 1.3. List menu example.

Different learning levels. This menu has the flexibility to allow for individualized contracts for different learning levels within the classroom. Because classrooms may have many ability levels, it might be necessary to contract students based on their ability or results from the pretesting of content. In which case, each student can contract for a certain number of points for their 100%.

Concept reinforcement. This menu allows for an in-depth study of the material. With the different levels of Bloom's revised taxonomy being represented, however, students who are at the early stages of learning the concepts can choose lower-level point value products to reinforce the basics before jumping into the higher level activities.

Variety. A list menu offers a larger variety of product choices. There is guaranteed to be a product of interest to everyone. (And if there isn't, there is always free choice!)

Limitations

One topic. If using the traditional challenge list format, this menu can only be used for one topic in depth, so that students cannot miss any specific content.

Cannot guarantee objectives. If the traditional challenge menu is used for more than one topic, it is possible for a student to not have to complete an activity for each objective, depending on the choices they make.

Preparation. Teachers need to have all materials ready at the beginning of the unit for students to be able to choose any of the activities on the list. This expectation requires a degree of advanced planning. (*Note*: This advanced preparation leads to low stress during the unit as all of the materials have already been gathered.)

Time Considerations

List menus usually are intended for shorter amounts of completion time—at the most, 2 weeks. (*Note*: Once you have assembled the materials, the preparation is minimal!)

20-50-80 Menus

"As you suggested, I used one of your 20-50-80 menus as homework to review equations of a line the week before we went into solving systems of equations. It was very easy for the students to understand and saved so much time at the beginning of the systems unit. I am going to use these more often."

—Algebra I teacher

Description

A 20-50-80 menu (see Figure 1.4; Magner, 2000), is a variation on a List menu, with a total of at least eight predetermined choices: no more than two choices with a point value of 20, at least four choices with a point value of 50, and at least two choices with a point value of 80. Choices are assigned these points based on the levels of Bloom's revised taxonomy. Choices with a point value of 20 represent the remember and understand levels, choices with a point value of 50 represent the apply and analyze levels, and choices with a point value of 80 represent the evaluate and create levels. All levels of choices carry different weights and have different expectations for completion time and effort. Students are expected to earn 100 points for a 100%. Students choose what combination of products they would like to complete to attain that point goal.

Benefits

Responsibility. With this menu, students have complete control over goals and their grade. (*Note*: This is not to say that it is acceptable for students to choose 70% as their goal. The expectation is always that the students will work to achieve or exceed the point goal for the menu.)

Guaranteed activity. This menu's design is set up in such a way that students must complete at least one activity at a higher level of Bloom's revised taxonomy to reach their point goal.

Grade-as-you-go. This menu requires that teachers grade products as the students complete them. Actively grading and providing immediate feedback are important so the students can alter their plans and choose to submit additional products to be sure they reach the point goal. Additionally, by grading-as-you-go, teachers will not have piles of products to grade once the menu is completed.

Low stress. This menu is one of the shortest menus. If students choose well and complete quality products, they could accomplish their goal by completing just two products. This menu is usually not as daunting as some of the longer, more complex menus. The 20-50-80 menu provides students a great introduction into the process of making choices.

Figure 1.4. 20-50-80 menu example.

Limitations

One topic. If this menu is used for more than one topic, it is possible for a student to not have to complete an activity for each objective, depending on the choices they make. Therefore, a 20-50-80 menu is limited in the number of topics it can assess.

Limited higher level thinking. Students could potentially complete only one activity at a higher level of thinking (although many students will complete more to allow themselves a "cushion" in case they do not earn full credit on a product.

Time Considerations

These menus are usually intended for a shorter amount of completion time—at the most, 2 weeks with students working outside of class, or one week, if class time is allowed for product completion.

Free Choice

> *"I try to bring in real-world applications for each concept we cover. Sometimes it might be the students simply answering, 'How does this apply to your life?' So, now I let them use the free-choice proposals and they can create something to show me the application of the material."*
>
> **—High school AP Chemistry teacher**

As a menu option, students may be offered the opportunity to submit a free choice for their teacher's consideration. Figure 1.5 shows two sample proposal forms that have been used many times successfully in my classroom. The form provided to students is based on the type of menu being presented. If using a target-based menu like the Tic-Tac-Toe or Meal menu, there is no need to submit a free-choice proposal form that includes the mention of points.

When implementing a menu that includes free choice, a copy of the appropriate free-choice proposal form should be given to each student when the menu is first introduced. The form should be discussed with the students, so they understand the expectations of proposing a free choice. If they do not want to make a proposal after you have discussed the menu

Name: _____   Teacher's Approval: _____

Free-Choice Proposal Form for Point-Based Menu

Points Requested:		Points Approved:	

Proposal Outline

1. What specific topic or idea will you learn about?

2. What criteria should be used to grade it? (Neatness, content, creativity, artistic value, etc.)

3. What will your product look like?

4. What materials will you need from the teacher to create this product?

Name: _____   Teacher's Approval: _____

Free-Choice Proposal Form for Menus

Proposal Outline

1. What specific topic or idea will you learn about?

2. What criteria should be used to grade it? (Neatness, content, creativity, artistic value, etc.)

3. What will your product look like?

4. What materials will you need from the teacher to create this product?

Figure 1.5. Free-choice proposal forms.

and its activities, the students can place unused forms in a designated place. I always had a box of blank proposal forms on the supply table in my classroom, so unused forms could be returned there. Some students may want to keep their free-choice proposal form "just in case"—you may be surprised who wants to submit a proposal form after hearing about the opportunity!

These proposal forms must be submitted before students begin working on their free choice. That way, the teacher knows what the students are working on, and the student knows the expectations for the product of choice. Once approved, the forms can be stapled to the student's menu sheet for reference. The students can refer to it as they develop their free choice, and when the grading takes place, the teacher can refer to the agreement for the "graded" features of the product.

Each part of the proposal form is important and needs to be discussed with students during the introductory discussion of the form.

- *Name/Teacher's approval.* It is very important that the student submits this form to the teacher. The teacher will carefully review all of the information, give it back to the student for clarification if needed, and then sign the top. Although not always possible, I preferred that the students discuss their forms with me, so we can both be clear about their ideas.

- *Points requested.* Only on the point-based menu proposal form, this is usually where negotiation takes place. Students will often submit their first free-choice request for a very high number of points (even the 100% goal). Students tend to equate the amount of time an activity or product will take with the amount of points it should earn. Unfortunately, the points are always based on the level of Bloom's taxonomy. A PowerPoint with a vocabulary word quiz would get minimal points although it may have taken a long time to create. If the students have not been exposed to the levels of Bloom's taxonomy, the assigning of points can be difficult to explain. Teachers can always refer to the popular "Bloom's Verbs" to help explain the difference between time and higher level activities.

- *Points approved.* Only on the point-based menu proposal form, this is the final decision recorded by the teacher once the point haggling is finished.

- *Proposal outline.* This is where the students will tell you everything about the product that they intend to complete. These questions should be completed in such a way that you can picture what they are planning on completing. These questions also show you that the students know what they are planning on completing as well.

○ *What specific topic or idea will you learn about?* Students need to be specific here, not just "science" or "writing." This response is where the students need look at the objectives or standards of the unit and choose which objective they would like to address through their product.

○ *What criteria should be used to grade it?* Although there are guidelines for all of the projects that the students might create, it is important for the students to explain what criteria are most important in its evaluation. The student may indicate that the product guideline being used for all of the predetermined product is fine; however, they may also want to add other criteria here.

○ *What will your product look like?* It is important that this response be as detailed as possible. If students cannot express what it will "look like," then they have probably not given their free choice enough thought.

○ *What materials will you need from the teacher to create this product?* This question is an important consideration. Sometimes students do not have the means to purchase items for their project. These materials can be negotiated as well, but if you ask what students may need, they often will develop even grander ideas for their free choice. This may also be a place for students to note any special equipment or technology needs they may have to create their product.

CHAPTER 2

How to Use Menus in the Classroom

Instructional menus can be used in different ways in the secondary classroom. To decide how to implement your choice menu, the following questions should be considered:

- How confident are your students in making choices and working independently?
- How much intellectually appropriate information is readily available for students to obtain on their own?
- How much prior knowledge of the topic being taught do the students have before the unit or lesson begins?

After considering the responses to these questions, there is a variety of ways to use menus.

Building Background Knowledge or Accessing Prior Knowledge

"I have students with so many different experiences—sometimes I spend a lot more time than I allotted to review and get everyone up to speed before we get started."

—Secondary social studies teacher

There are many ways to use menus in the classroom. One way that is often overlooked is using menus to review or build background knowledge or access prior knowledge before a unit begins. Using menus this way is beneficial when students have had exposure to upcoming content in the past, perhaps during the previous year's instruction or through life experiences. Many high school students have had preliminary exposure to the basic information needed in their classes. However, students may not remember the details of the content at the depth needed to proceed with the upcoming unit immediately. A shorter menu covering the background or previous year's objectives can be provided the week prior to the new unit. This way, students have the opportunity to recall and engage with the information in a meaningful way, while not using valuable class time during the first day of a new unit to do so. Because the teacher knows that the students have covered the content in the past, the students should be able to work independently on the menu by engaging their prior knowledge. Students work on products from the selected menu as anchor activities and/or homework throughout the week preceding the new unit, with all products being submitted prior to the upcoming unit's initiation. By using menus in this manner, students have been thinking about the upcoming unit for a week and are ready to investigate the topic further. Students are prepared to take their knowledge to a deeper level on the first day of instruction, conserving that much-needed instruction time.

Enrichment and Supplemental Activities

"Just because my students are teenagers doesn't mean they do not need enrichment; the problem is finding time. My curriculum is so packed, and I had always had trouble getting any in. I tried using an enrichment menu for the body systems since I thought we might have enough time. The students really enjoyed it; they seemed to make time for it. I need to use more."

—High school biology teacher

Using menus for enrichment and supplementary activities is the most common way of implementing menus in the classroom. Many teachers who want to "dip their toes" in the menu pool will begin by using menus this way because it does not directly impact their current teaching style. The students usually do not have much background knowledge, and information about the topic may not be readily available to all students while working on the menu.

When using menus for enrichment or supplemental activities, the teacher should introduce the menu and the choice activities at the beginning of a unit—before any instruction has taken place. The teacher then will progress through the content at the normal rate using their curricular materials, periodically allowing class and/or homework time throughout the unit for students to work on their menu choices to supplement a deeper understanding of the lessons being taught. Although it may seem counterintuitive to provide enrichment before any instruction takes place, it facilitates a need to know, or an epistemic curiosity (Litman et al., 2005).

This method incorporates an immediate use for the content the teacher is providing. For example, at the beginning of a unit, the teacher introduces the menu with the explanation that students may not have all of the knowledge to complete their choices yet. As instruction progresses, however, more content will be provided, and the students will be prepared to work on new choices. If students want to work ahead, they certainly can find the information on their own, but this is not required. Gifted students often see the ability to work ahead as a challenge and will begin to investigate concepts mentioned in the menu before the teacher has discussed them. Other students may start to develop questions about the concepts and then are ready to ask their questions when the teacher covers the new material. This "advance investigation" helps build an immense pool of background knowledge and potential content questions before the topic is even discussed in the classroom. As teachers, we constantly fight the battle of having students read ahead or "come to class prepared for discussion." By introducing a menu at the beginning of a unit and allowing students to complete products as instruction progresses, we encourage the students to naturally investigate the information and come to class prepared without having to make preparation a separate requirement.

Mainstream Instructional/Flipped Classroom Activities

"On your suggestion, I tried using a menu with my geometry unit since I had 3 days of instruction that the students knew well and could work on independently. They really responded to the independence."

—Secondary math teacher

Another option for using menus in the classroom is to offer a choice between certain in-class curricular activities. For example, after students have obtained basic instruction outside of the classroom (through research, videos, or other sources), students can be offered a menu of choices to organize their activities and facilitate their learning during class time. The students spend class time working on the activities on their menus; the teacher spends class time facilitating the choices that students have selected.

If teachers follow a more traditional model, menus can be used when students have some limited background knowledge about the content and appropriate information is readily available for them among their classroom resources. The teacher would select which aspects of the content must be directly taught to the students and which could be appropriately learned and reinforced through product menu activities. The unit is then designed using both formal instructional lessons and specific menu days during which the students will use the menu to strengthen the prior knowledge they already have learned, apply the new information, or extend recently presented information in a differentiated way. For this use of menus to be effective, the teacher must feel very comfortable with the students' prior knowledge level and their readiness to work independently.

Mini-Lessons

"I have so many different levels in my classroom, using menus with mini-lessons has been a life saver. I actually can work with small groups and everyone else doesn't run wild!"

—Secondary math teacher

Another option for menu use is the use of mini-lessons, with the menus driving the accompanying classroom activities. This method is best when most of the students have similar degrees of knowledge about the topic. The teacher designs short 10–15-minute mini-lessons, in which students quickly review fundamental concepts that already are familiar to them as well as experience new content in a brief, concise way. After these short mini-lessons, students can select an activity on the menu to demonstrate their understanding of the new concept.

A topic list can work well with mini-lessons. The menu can be designed so the topics along the left side of the menu represent one mini-lesson per day (or per content). Using menus in this way shortens the amount of time teachers use the guided practice aspect of the lesson, so all instruction and examples should be carefully selected. The benefit of using menus with mini-lessons is the teacher gets to avoid the one-size-fits-all independent practice portion of the lesson. If a few students still struggle after the mini-lesson, they can be pulled into a small group while the other students work on their choices from the menu.

An important consideration when using menus this way is the independence level of the students. For mini-lesson menus to be effective, students will need to be able to work independently for up to 30 minutes after the mini-lesson. Students are often interested in the product they have chosen, so this may not be a critical issue, but it is still one worth mentioning as teachers consider how they would like to use various menus in their classroom.

CHAPTER 3

Guidelines for Products

"It was different being able to do something other than a drawing or folded paper. I haven't made a video for school in years!"

—High school chemistry student

This chapter outlines the different types of products used in the included menus as well as guidelines and expectations for each. It is crucial that students know the expectations of a product before they choose to work on it. By discussing these expectations before the students begin and having the information readily available, you will save frustration on everyone's part.

$1 Contract

"I really appreciate the $1 form. It kept me from having to run to [craft store] and spend $60 on felt and glitter and all of the other things we normally have to buy for projects."

—Parent of one of my students when asked for feedback on a recent menu

Consideration should be given to the cost of creating the products in any menu. The resources available to students vary within a classroom, and students should not be evaluated on the amount of materials they can purchase to make a product look glittery. The menus in this book are designed to equalize the resources students have available. For most products, the materials are available for under a dollar and can often be found in a teacher's classroom as part of their supplies. If a product would require materials from the student, the $1 contract is included as part of the product's guideline. This contract is an important aspect of the explanation of the product. By limiting the amount of money a child can spend, it creates an equality of resources for all students. This limitation also encourages a more creative product. When students are limited by the amount of materials they can readily purchase, they often have to use materials from home in new and unique ways. Figure 3.1 is a sample $1 contract that I have used many times with various products.

The Products

Table 3.1 contains a list of the products used in this book. These products were chosen for their flexibility in meeting learning preferences as well as being popular products most students have experienced and teachers may already use in their classroom. They have been arranged by learning preference—visual, kinesthetic, or auditory.

Each menu has been designed to include products from all of the learning preferences. Some of the products may be listed under more than one area depending on how they are presented or implemented (and some of the best products cross over between areas). The specific expectations (guidelines) for all of the products are presented in an easy-to-read card format that can be reproduced for students. This format is convenient for students to have in front of them when they work on their projects.

Product Frustrations

"One of the biggest reasons I haven't used more than one product at a time is that I have to constantly reexplain what I want for it. Even if the students write it down, it doesn't mean they won't pester me about it all week."

—English I teacher

```
┌─────────────────────────────────────────────────────────────────────┐
│                         $1 Contract                                   │
│                                                                       │
│  I did not spend more than $1.00 on my _____ .    │
│                                                                       │
│                                                                       │
│  _____    _____ │
│           Student Signature                         Date              │
│                                                                       │
│  My child, _____ , did not spend more than $1.00  │
│  on the product they created.                                         │
│                                                                       │
│                                                                       │
│  _____    _____ │
│           Parent Signature                          Date              │
└─────────────────────────────────────────────────────────────────────┘
```

Figure 3.1. $1 contract.

One of the biggest frustrations that accompany the use of a variety of menu products is the barrage of questions about the products themselves. Students can become so engulfed in the products and the criteria for creating them that they do not focus on the content being synthesized. This focus on products is especially true when menus are introduced to students.

Students can spend an exorbitant amount of time asking the teacher about the products mentioned on the menu. When this interrogation begins, what should have been a 10–15-minute menu introduction turns into 45–50 minutes of discussion about product expectations—without any discussion of the content!

During this discussion, teachers may consider showing students examples of the product(s) from the previous year. Although this can be helpful, it can also lead to additional frustration on the part of both the teacher and the students. Some students may not feel that they can produce a product as nice, as big, as special, or as (you fill in the blank) as the example. Alternatively, when shown an example, students might interpret that the teacher would like something exactly like the example they showed to students. To avoid this situation, I would propose that when using examples, students are shown a "blank" example that demonstrates how to create the shell of the product. For example, if a window pane is needed, students might be shown a blank piece of paper that the teacher has divided into six panes. The students can then take the "skeleton" of

Table 3.1
Products

Visual	Kinesthetic	Auditory/Oral
Acrostic	Board Game	Board Game
Advertisement	Book Cover	Children's Book
Book Cover	Bulletin Board Display	Class Game
Brochure/Pamphlet	Card Sort	Classroom Model
Cartoon/Comic Strip	Class Game	Commercial
Children's Book	Classroom Model	Game Show
Choose Your Own	Collage	Interview
Adventure	Commercial	News Report
Collage	Concentration Cards	Play
Crossword Puzzle	Cross Cut Model	Presentation of Created
Diary/Journal	Diorama	Product
Drawing	Flipbook	PowerPoint–Speaker
Essay	Folded Quiz Book	Puppet Show
Folded Quiz Book	Game Show	Speech
Greeting Card	Mobile	Song/Rap
Instruction Card	Model	Student-Taught Lesson
Graphic Novel	Mural	You Be the Person
Greeting Card	Museum Exhibit	Presentation
Letter/E-mail	Play	Video
Map	Product Cube	
Mind Map	Puppet	
Newspaper Article	Quiz Board	
Poster	Scrapbook	
Power Point–Stand	Science Experiment	
Alone	Student-Taught Lesson	
Questionnaire	Three-Dimensional	
Quiz	Timeline	
Recipe	Trading Cards	
Scrapbook	Trophy	
Social Media Profile	Video	
Story	WebQuest	
Three Facts and a Fib		
Trading Cards		
Venn Diagram		
WebQuest		
Window Pane		
Worksheet		

the product and make it their own as they create their version of the window pane using their information.

Product Guidelines

"Wow. You know how great these are . . . how much time they will save?"

—A group of teachers, when presented with a page of products guidelines for their classroom

Most frustrations associated with the varied products placed on menus can be addressed proactively using standardized, predetermined product guidelines. These guidelines should be shared with students prior to them creating any products. Although these guidelines may look like "mini-rubrics," they are designed in a generic way, such that any time throughout the school year that students select a product, that product's guidelines will apply.

A beneficial side effect of using set guidelines for a product is the security the guideline creates in the choice-making process. Students are often reticent to try something new, as doing so requires taking a risk. Traditionally, when students select products, they ask questions about creating the product, hope they remember all of the details, and submit the product for grading. It can be quite a shock when the students receive the product back and realize that their product was not complete or was not what the teacher expected. As you can imagine, students may not want to take the risk on something new the next time. Instead, they may prefer to stick to what they know and be successful. Using standardized product guidelines, students can begin to feel secure in their choice before they start working on a new product. Without this security, students tend to stay within their comfort zone.

Sharing the Product Guidelines

> *"Wow! It's already done for us."*
>
> —A group of teachers at staff development after
> discovering the product guidelines pages

The guidelines for all of the products used on the menus in this book, as well as some potential free-choice options, are included in an easy-to-read card format (see Figure 3.2). Once the topic menu has been selected, there are many ways to share this information with students. There is no one "right way" to share the product guideline information with your students. The method you select depends on your students' abilities and needs.

For students who are independent and responsible, teachers may duplicate and distribute all of the product guidelines pages to students at the beginning of the year. Students can glue them into the front of their notebooks or punch holes and place them in binders. By providing them in advance, each student has their copy to use while working on menu products during the school year.

If teachers prefer a more controlled method, class sets can be created. These sets can be created by gluing each product guideline onto a separate index card, hole punching the corner of each card, and placing all of the cards on a metal ring. These ring sets can be put in a central location or at a supply table where students can borrow and return them as they work on their products. Using a ring also allows for the addition of products as they are introduced. Additionally, the rings and index cards can be color-coded based on learning preference, encouraging students to step out of their comfort zone during free choice.

Some teachers prefer to expose students to products as students experience them on their menus. In this case, product guidelines from the menu currently assigned can be enlarged and posted on a bulletin board or wall for easy access during classroom work. Some teachers may choose to reproduce each menu's specific product guidelines on the back of the menu.

No matter which method teachers select to share the product guideline information with the students, teachers will save themselves a lot of time and frustration by having the product guidelines available for student reference (e.g., "Look at your product guidelines—I think that will answer your question").

Acrostic	Advertisement	Board Game
• Must be at least 8.5" by 11" • Must be neatly written or typed • Target word must be written down the left side of the paper • Each descriptive phrase chosen must begin with one of the letters from the target word • Each descriptive phrase chosen must be related to the target word • Name must be written on the acrostic	• Must be at least 8.5" by 11" • Must include a meaningful slogan • Must include a color picture of item or service • Must include price, if appropriate • Could be developed electronically • Name must be written on the advertisement	• Must have at least four thematic game pieces • Must have at least 25 colored/thematic squares • Must have at least 20 question/activity cards • Must have thematic title on the game • Must have a complete set of rules for playing the game • Must be at least the size of an open file folder • Name must be written on the front of the board game

Book Cover	Brochure/Pamphlet	Bulletin Board Display

Must include five parts:
• **Front cover**—title, author, image
• **Cover inside flap**—paragraph summary of the book
• **Back inside flap**—brief biography of author with at least five details
• **Back cover**—editorial comments about book
• **Spine**—title and author
  » May be placed on actual book, but not necessary
  » Name must be written on the book cover
	• Must be at least 8.5" by 11"
	• Must be in three-fold format
	• Front fold must have the title and picture
	• Must have both pictures and information
	• Information must be in paragraph form with at least five facts included
	• Bibliography or sources must be provided if needed
	• Can be created on computer
	• Any pictures from the Internet must have proper credit
	• Name must be written on the cover of the brochure
		• Must fit within assigned space on bulletin board or wall
		• Must include at least 10 details
		• Must have a title
		• Must have at least five different elements (posters, papers, questions, etc.)
		• Must have at least one interactive element that engages the reader
		• Name must be written on the bottom of the display

Card Sort	Cartoon/Comic Strip	Children's Book
• Must have at least 16 total cards • Must have at least five cards in each column • Can have more than two columns if appropriate • Answer key must be submitted • All cards must be submitted in a carrying bag • Name must be written on the carrying bag	• Must be at least 8.5" by 11" • Must have at least six cells • Must have meaningful dialogue that addresses the task • Must have color • Name must be written on the bottom of the cartoon or comic strip	• Must have a cover with book's title and student's name as author • Must have at least 10 pages • Each page must have an illustration to accompany the story • Must be neatly written or typed • Can be developed on the computer

Figure 3.2. Product guidelines.

Class Game	Classroom Model	Collage
• Game must allow all class members to participate • Must have only a few, easy-to-understand rules • Must be inventive or a new variation on a current game • Must have multiple question opportunities • Must provide answer key before the game is played • Name must be written on the answer key • The game must be approved by the teacher before being scheduled for play	• Must use everyone in the class in the model • Must not take longer than 2 minutes to arrange everyone • Students must be able to understand the part they play in the model • After the model is created, the explanation of the model must not take longer than 2 minutes • Must submit a paragraph that shares how the arrangement of students represents the concept being modeled • Name must be written on the paragraph submitted	• Must be at least 8.5" by 11" • Pictures must be neatly cut from magazines or newspapers (no clip art) • Must label items as required in task • Name must be written on the bottom of the collage
Commercial/Infomercial	**Concentration Cards**	**Cross Cut Model/Diagram**
• Must be between 1 and 3 minutes • Script must be turned in before commercial is presented • May be either live or recorded beforehand based on teacher discretion • Must have props or some form of costume(s) • Can include more than one person • Name must be written on the script	• Must have at least 20 index cards (10 matching sets) • Can use both pictures and words • Information must be placed on just one side of each card • Must include an answer key that shows the matches • All cards must be submitted in a carrying bag • Name must be written on the carrying bag	• Must include a scale to show the relationship between product and the actual item • Must include details about each layer • If creating a model, must also meet the criteria of a model • If creating a diagram, must also meet the criteria of a poster • Name must be written on the model
Crossword Puzzle	**Diary/Journal**	**Diorama**
• Must have at least 20 significant words or phrases included • Clues must be appropriate • Must include puzzle and answer key • Can be created using a computer • Name must be written on the crossword puzzle	• Must be neatly written or typed • Must include the appropriate number of entries • Must include a date for each entry if appropriate • Must be written in first person • Name must be written on the diary or journal	• Must be at least 4" by 5" by 8" • Must be self-standing • All interior space must be covered with relevant pictures and information • Name must be written on the back in permanent ink • Must submit a signed $1 contract • Informational/title card must be attached to diorama

Figure 3.2. Continued.

Drawing	E-mail	Essay
• Must be at least 8.5" by 11" • Must show what is requested in the task statement • Must include color • Must be neatly drawn by hand • Must have title • Name must be written on the back	• Must be neatly written or typed • Must cover the specific topic of the task • Must include standard to, from, and subject • Must include appropriate (but fictitious) e-mail addresses of sender and recipient • Must be signed with custom signature from sender	• Must be neatly written or typed • Must cover the specific topic in detail • Must be at least three paragraphs • Must include bibliography or sources if appropriate • Name must be written in the heading of the essay
Flipbook	**Folded Quiz Book**	**Game Show**
• Must be at least 8.5" by 11" folded in half • All information or opinions must be supported by facts • Must be created with the correct number of flaps cut into the top • Color is optional • Name must be written on the back of the flipbook	• Must be at least 8.5" by 11" • Must have at least 10 questions • Must be created with the correct number of flaps cut into the top • Questions must be written or typed neatly on upper flaps • Answers must be written or typed neatly inside each flap • Color is optional • Name must be written on the back of the quiz book	• Must have an emcee or host • Must have at least two contestants • Must have at least one regular round and a bonus round • Questions must be content specific • Props can be used, but are not mandatory • Name must be written on the questions used in the game
Greeting Card	**Instruction Card**	**Interview**
Must include four parts: • **Front**—colored pictures, words optional • **Front inside**—personal note related to topic • **Back inside**—greeting or saying, must meet menu task • **Back outside**—logo, publisher, and price for card » Name must be written on the back of the card	• Must be no larger than 5" by 8" • Must be created on heavy paper or card • Must be neatly written or typed • Must use color drawings • Must provide instructions stated in the task • Name must be written on the back of the card	• Must have at least eight questions important to the topic being studied • Person chosen for interview must be an "expert" and qualified to provide answers based on product criteria • Questions and answers must be neatly written or typed • Name must be written on the interview questions

Figure 3.2. Continued.

Letter	Map	Mind Map
• Must be neatly written or typed • Must use proper letter format • Must have at least three paragraphs • Must follow type of letter stated in the menu (friendly, persuasive, informational) • Name must be included in the letter in a meaningful way	• Must be at least 8.5" by 11" • Must contain accurate information • Must include at least 10 relevant locations • Must include compass rose, legend, scale, key • Name must be written on the back of the map	• Must be at least 8.5" by 11" • Must use unlined paper • Must have one central idea • Must follow the "no more than four rule": There must be no more than four words coming from any one word • Must be neatly written or developed using a computer program • Name must be written on the mind map

Mobile	Model	Mural
• Must contain at least 10 pieces of related information • Must include color and pictures • Must include at least three layers of hanging information • Must be able to hang in a balanced way • Name must be written on one of the cards hanging from the mobile	• Must be at least 8" by 8" by 12" • Parts of model must be labeled • Must be in scale when appropriate • Must include a title card • Name must be permanently written on model	• Must be at least 22" x 54" • Must have at least five pieces of important information • Must have colored pictures • Words are optional, but must have title • Name must be written on the back of the mural in a permanent way

Museum Exhibit	News Report	Newspaper Article
• Must have title for exhibit • Must include at least five "artifacts" • Each artifact must be labeled with a neatly written card • Exhibit must fit within the size assigned • Must submit a signed $1 contract • No expensive or irreplaceable objects may be used in the display • Name must be written on a label card in the exhibit	• Must address the who, what, where, when, why, and how of the topic • Script of news report must be turned in with product, or before if performance will be "live" • May be either live or recorded beforehand based on teacher discretion • Name announced during the performance and clearly written on script	• Must be informational in nature • Must follow standard newspaper format • Must include picture with caption that supports article • Must contain at least three paragraphs • Must be neatly written or typed • Name must be written at the top of the article

Figure 3.2. Continued.

Play/Skit	Poster	PowerPoint–Stand Alone
• Must be between 3 and 5 minutes • Script must be turned in before play is presented • May be presented to an audience or recorded for future showing to audience based on teacher discretion • Must have props or some form of costume • Can include more than one person • Name must be written on the script that is submitted with the play	• Must be the size of a standard poster board • Must contain at least five pieces of important information • Must have title • Must have both words and pictures • Name must be written on the back of the poster in a permanent way • Bibliography or sources must be included as needed	• Must contain at least 10 informational slides • Must not have more than 10 words per page • Slides must have color and no more than one graphic per page • Animations are optional but must not distract from the information being presented • Bibliography or sources must be included as needed • Name must be written on the first slide of the PowerPoint
PowerPoint–Speaker	**Project Cube**	**Puppet**
• Must contain at least 10 informational slides • Must not have more than two words per page • Slides must have color and no more than one graphic per page • Animations are optional but must not distract from information being presented • Presentation must be timed and flow with the speech being given • Name must be written on the first slide of the PowerPoint	• All six sides of the cube must be filled with information as stated in the task • Must be neatly written or typed • Name must be printed neatly on the bottom of one of the sides of the cube • Must be submitted flat for grading	• Puppet must be handmade and must have a movable mouth • A list of supplies used to make the puppet must be turned in with the puppet • Must submit a signed $1 contract • If used in a puppet show, all play criteria must be met as well • Name must be written on the inside of the puppet where it can be seen
Questionnaire	**Quiz**	**Quiz Board**
• Must be neatly written or typed • Must contain at least 10 questions with possible answers • Must contain at least one answer that requires a written response • Questions must be helpful to gathering information on the topic begin studied • If questionnaire is to be used, at least 15 people must provide answers • Name must be written at the top of the questionnaire	• Must be at least a half sheet of paper • Must be neatly written or typed • Must cover the specific topic in detail • Must include at least five questions, including at least one short answer question • Must have at least one graphic • An answer key must be turned in with the quiz • Name must be written on the top of the quiz	• Must have at least five questions • Must have at least five answers, although there could be more for distractors • Must use a system with lights to facilitate self-checking • Name must be written in a permanent way on the back of the quiz board

Figure 3.2. Continued.

Recipe/Recipe Card	Scrapbook	Social Media Profile
• Must be written neatly or typed on a piece of paper or an index card • Must have a list of ingredients with measurements for each • Must have numbered steps that explain how to make the recipe • Name must be written at the top of the recipe card	• Cover of scrapbook must have a meaningful title and student's name • Must have at least five themed pages • Each page must have at least one meaningful picture • All photos and pictures must have captions • Bibliography or sources must be included as needed	• Must include profile picture • Must include other relevant information about the "person" • Must include at least five status updates with comments from "friends" • Can be created electronically or in poster format • Name must be included on the social media profile in a creative way
Song/Rap	**Speech**	**Story**
• Must be original (not found online or sung by anyone else before) • Words or lyrics must make sense • May be either live or recorded beforehand based on teacher discretion • Written words must be turned in before performance or with taped song • Must be at least 2 minutes in length • Name must be written on the written words submitted with the song or rap	• Must be at least 2 minutes in length • Must not be read from written paper • Note cards can be used • Written speech must be turned in before speech is presented • May be either live or recorded beforehand based on teacher discretion • Voice must be clear, loud, and easy to understand • Name must be written on the written speech	• Must be neatly written or typed • Must have all elements of a well-written story (setting, characters, conflict, rising action, and resolution) • Must be appropriate length to allow for story elements • Name must be written on the story
Three-Dimensional Timeline	**Three Facts and a Fib**	**Trading Cards**
• Must not be bigger than a standard-size poster board • Must be divided into equal time units • Must contain at least 10 important dates • Must have at least two sentences explaining why each date is important • Must have a meaningful object securely attached beside each date to represent that date • Objects must be creative • Must be able to explain how each object represents each date or event • Name must be written at the bottom of the timeline	• Can be handwritten, typed, or created in PowerPoint • Must include exactly four statements: three true statements (facts) and one false statement (fib) • False statement must not be obvious • Brief paragraph must accompany product that explains why the fib is false • Name must be written on the product	• Must include at least 10 cards • Each card must be at least 3" by 5" • Each card must have a colored picture • Must contain at least three facts on the subject of the card • Cards must have information on both sides • All cards must be submitted in a carrying bag • Name must be written on the carrying bag

Figure 3.2. Continued.

Trophy	Venn Diagram	Video
• Must be at least 6" tall • Must have a base with the name of the person getting the trophy and the name of the award written neatly or typed on it • Top of trophy must be appropriate and represent the nature of the award • Name must be written on the bottom of the award • Must be an original trophy (avoid reusing a trophy from home)	• Must be at least 8.5" by 11" • Diagram shapes must be thematic (rather than just circles) and neatly drawn • Must have a title for entire diagram and a title for each section • Must have at least six items in each section of the diagram • Name must be written neatly on the back of the paper	• Must use video format • Must submit a written plan or story board with project • Students must arrange their own way to record their video or allow teacher **at least** 3 days notice for help in obtaining a way to record the video • Must cover pertinent information • Name must be written on the label or in the file name
WebQuest	**Window Pane**	**Worksheet**
• Must quest through at least five high-quality websites • Websites must be linked in the document • Can be submitted using a word processor or PowerPoint • Must contain at least three questions for each website • Must address the topic • Name must be written on the WebQuest or in the file name	• Must be at least 8.5" by 11" on unlined paper • Must contain at least six squares • Each square must include both a picture and words • All pictures must be both creative and meaningful • Must be neatly written or typed • Name must be written on the bottom right hand corner of the front of the window pane	• Must be 8.5" by 11" • Must be neatly written or typed • Must cover the specific topic or question in detail • Must be creative in design • Must have at least one graphic • An answer key must be turned in with the worksheet • Name must be written at the top of the worksheet
You Be the Person Presentation		
• Presenter must take on the role of the person • Must cover at least five important facts about the life or achievements of the person • Must be between 2 and 4 minutes in length • Script must be turned in before information is presented • Must be presented to an audience with the ability to answer questions while in character • Must have props or some form of costume • Name must be written on the script		

Figure 3.2. Continued.

CHAPTER 4

Rubrics

"One rubric—and I can grade everything? Now we are talking!"

—Group of secondary teachers

The most common reason teachers feel uncomfortable with menus is the need for fair and equal grading. If all of the students create the same product, teachers feel these products are easier to grade than 100 different products, none of which looks like any other. The great equalizer for hundreds of different products is a generic rubric that can evaluate the important qualities of an excellent product.

All-Purpose Rubric

Figure 4.1 is an example of a rubric that has been classroom tested with various menus. This rubric can be used with any point value activity presented in a menu, as there are five criteria, and the columns represent full points, half points, and no points. For example, if a student completes a 20-point product, each criterion would be worth four points (full

All-Purpose Rubric   Name: _____

Criteria	Excellent (Full Credit)	Good (Half Credit)	Poor (No Credit)	Self
Content Is the content of the product well chosen?	Content chosen represents the best choice for the product. Information or graphics are well chosen and related to content.	Information or graphics are related to content, but are not the best choice for the product.	Information or graphics present do not appear related to the topic or task.	
Completeness Is everything included in the product?	All information needed is included. Product meets the product guideline criteria and the criteria of the menu task.	Some important information is missing. Product meets the product guideline criteria and the criteria of the menu task.	Most important information is missing. The product does not meet the task or does not meet the product criteria.	
Creativity Is the product original?	Presentation of information is from a new and original perspective. Graphics are original. Product includes elements of fun and interest.	Presentation of information is from a new perspective. Graphics are not original. Product has elements of fun and interest.	There is no evidence of new thoughts or perspectives in the product, or any part of the product was plagiarized.	
Correctness Is all of the information included correct?	All information presented is correct and accurate.		Any portion of the information presented in product is incorrect.	
Communication Is the information in the product well communicated?	All information is neat and easy to read. Product is in appropriate format and shows significant effort. Oral presentation was easy to understand and presented with fluency.	Most (80%) of the product is neat and easy to read. Product is in appropriate format and shows significant effort. Oral presentation was easy to understand, with some fluency.	More than 20% of the product is not neat and easy to read, or the product is not in the appropriate format. It does not show significant effort. Oral presentation was not fluent or easy to understand.	
			Total Grade:	

Figure 4.1. All-purpose rubric.

© Prufrock Press Inc. • *Differentiating Instruction With Menus: Physics* • Grades 9–12

points), two points (half points), and zero (no points). Although Tic-Tac-Toe and Meal menus are not point based, this rubric can also be used to grade products from these menus. Teachers simply assign 100 points to each of the three products on the Tic-Tac-Toe and Meal menus. Then each criterion would be worth 20 points, and the all-purpose rubric can be used to grade each product individually.

There are different ways that teachers can share this rubric with students. Some teachers prefer to provide it when they present a menu to students. The rubric can be reproduced on the back of the menu along with its guidelines. The rubric can also be given to students at the beginning of the year with the product guideline cards. This way, students will always know the expectations as they complete projects throughout the school year. Some teachers prefer to keep a master copy of the rubric for themselves and post an enlarged copy on a bulletin board. If teachers wanted to share the rubric with parents, they could provide a copy for parents during back-to-school night, open house, or on private teacher web pages so that the parents will understand how teachers will grade their children's products.

No matter how teachers choose to share the rubric with students, the first time students see this rubric, it should be explained in detail, especially the last column, titled "Self." It is imperative that students self-evaluate their products. The Self column can provide a unique perspective on the product as it is being graded. *Note*: This rubric was designed to be specific enough that students will understand the criteria the teacher is seeking, but general enough that they can still be as creative as they like in the creation of their product.

Student-Taught Lessons and Oral Presentations

Although the all-purpose rubric can be used for all of the activities included on the menus in this book, there are two occasions that seem to warrant a special rubric: student-taught lessons and oral presentations. These are unique situations, with many fine details that must be considered to create a quality product.

Although valuable for both the student "teachers" and those in audience, student-taught lessons are not commonly used in the physics classroom. Secondary math curriculum is already packed with information, and turning class time over to students should only be done if it will benefit everyone involved; therefore, it can cause stress for both students and teachers. Teachers often would like to allow students to teach their fellow classmates but are concerned about quality lessons and may not feel comfortable with the grading aspect of the assignment. Rarely do students understand all of the components that go into designing an effective lesson. This student-taught lesson rubric (see Figure 4.2) helps focus the student on the important aspects of a well-designed lesson and allows teachers to make the evaluation a little more subjective.

Another situation which often needs clarification and focus to assist with time management is oral presentations. There are two rubrics included to assist with this process: one for the evaluation of the speaker by the teacher (see Figure 4.3) and one for feedback from the students (see Figure 4.4). A rubric is included for feedback from the students to encourage active participation on the part of the student observers. This student feedback is always meant to be given in a positive manner. When used with my students, they seemed to value their peers' feedback more than the rubric I gave them with the grades.

Student-Taught Lesson Rubric   Name: _____

Parts of Lesson	Excellent	Good	Fair	Poor	Self
Prepared and Ready All materials and lesson ready at the start of class period, from warm-up to conclusion of lesson.	10 Everything is ready to present.	6 Lesson is present, but small amount of scrambling.	3 Lesson is present, but major scrambling.	0 No lesson ready or missing major components.	
Understanding Presenter(s) understands the material well. Students understand information presented.	20 All information is correct and in correct format.	12 Presenter understands; 25% of students do not.	4 Presenter understands; 50% of students do not.	0 Presenter is confused.	
Complete Includes all significant information from section or topic.	15 Includes all important information.	10 Includes most important information.	2 Includes less than 50% of the important information.	0 Information is not related.	
Practice Includes some way for students to practice the information presented.	20 Practice present; was well chosen.	10 Practice present; can be applied effectively.	5 Practice present; not related or best choice.	0 No practice or students are confused.	
Interest/Fun Most of the class was involved, interested, and participating.	15 Everyone interested and participating.	10 75% actively participating.	5 Less than 50% actively participating.	0 Everyone off task.	
Creativity Information presented in an imaginative way.	20 Wow, creative! I never would have thought of that!	12 Good ideas!	5 Some good pieces but general instruction.	0 No creativity; all lecture, notes, or worksheet.	

Your Topic/Objective:

Comments:

Don't forget: All copy requests and material requests must be made at least 24 hours in advance.

Figure 4.2. Student-taught lesson rubric.

Oral Presentation Rubric

	Excellent	Good	Fair	Poor	Self
Content—Complete The presentation included everything it should.	**30** Presentation included all of the important information about the topic being presented.	**20** Presentation covered most of the important information, but one key idea was missing.	**10** Presentation covered some of the important information, but more than one key idea was missing.	**0** Presentation included some information, but it was trivial or fluff.	
Content—Correct All of the information presented was accurate.	**30** All of the information presented was accurate.	**20** All of the information presented was correct with a few unintentional errors that were quickly corrected.	**10** Most of the information presented was correct, but there were a few errors.	**0** The information presented was not correct.	
Content—Consistency Speaker stayed on topic during the presentation.	**10** Presenter stayed on topic 100% of the time.	**7** Presenter stayed on topic 90–99% of the time.	**4** Presenter stayed on topic 80–89% of the time.	**0** It was hard to tell what the topic was.	
Prop Speaker had at least one prop that was directly related to the presentation.	**20** Presenter had the prop, and it complemented the presentation.	**12** Presenter had a prop, but it was not the best choice.	**4** Presenter had a prop, but there was no clear reason for its choice.	**0** No prop.	
Flow Speaker knew the presentation well, so the words were well-spoken and flowed well together.	**10** Presentation flowed well. Speaker did not stumble over words.	**7** Some flow problems, but they did not distract from information.	**4** Some flow problems interrupted presentation; presenter seemed flustered.	**0** Constant flow problems; information was not presented in a way it could be understood.	
				Total Grade: (100)	

Figure 4.3. Oral presentation rubric.

Topic: _____   **Student's Name:** _____

On a scale of 1–10, rate the following areas:

	Your Ranking	
Content (Depth of information. How well did the speaker know their information? Was the information correct? Could the speaker answer questions?)	☐	Give one specific reason why you gave this number.
Flow (Did the presentation flow smoothly? Did the speaker appear confident and ready to speak?)	☐	Give one specific reason why you gave this number.
Prop (Did the speaker explain the prop they chose? Did the choice seem logical? Was it the best choice?)	☐	Give one specific reason why you gave this number.

Comments: Below, write two specific things that you think the presenter did well.

Topic: _____   **Student's Name:** _____

On a scale of 1–10, rate the following areas:

	Your Ranking	
Content (Depth of information. How well did the speaker know their information? Was the information correct? Could the speaker answer questions?)	☐	Give one specific reason why you gave this number.
Flow (Did the presentation flow smoothly? Did the speaker appear confident and ready to speak?)	☐	Give one specific reason why you gave this number.
Prop (Did the speaker explain the prop they chose? Did the choice seem logical? Was it the best choice?)	☐	Give one specific reason why you gave this number.

Comments: Below, write two specific things that you think the presenter did well.

Figure 4.4. Student feedback rubric.

PART II

The Menus

How to Use the Menu Pages

Each menu in this section has:
- an introduction page for the teacher that includes the answers to any calculations included on the menu,
- the content menu, and
- any specific activities mentioned in the menu.

Introduction Pages

The introduction pages are meant to provide an overview of each menu. They are divided into five areas.
- *Objectives Covered Through the Menu and Activities.* This area will list all of the instructional objectives that the menu can address. Although all of the objectives integrated into the menus correlate to state and national standards, these targets will be stated in a generic, teacher-friendly way. Menus are arranged in such a way that if students complete the guidelines outlined in the instructions for the menu, all of these objectives will be covered.

- *Materials Needed by Students for Completion.* For each menu, it is expected that the teacher will provide, or students will have access to, the following materials:
  ○ lined paper,
  ○ blank 8.5" by 11" white paper,
  ○ glue, and
  ○ colored pencils or markers.

  The introduction page also includes a list of additional materials that may be needed by students as they complete the menu. Students do have the choice of the menu items they can complete, so it is possible that the teacher will not need all of these materials for every student.
- *Special Notes on the Use of This Menu.* Some menus allow students to choose to present products to their classmates, build items out of recycled materials, or build quiz boards. This section will outline any special tips on managing products that may require more time, supplies, or space. This section will also share any tips to consider for a particular activity.
- *Time Frame.* Each menu has its ideal time frame based on its structure, but all need at least one week to complete. Menus that assess more objectives are better suited to more than 2 weeks. This section will give you an overview of the best time frame for completing the entire menu, as well as options for shorter time periods. If teachers do not have time to devote to a whole menu, they certainly can choose the 1–2-day option for any menu topic students are currently studying.
- *Suggested Forms.* This section contains a list of the rubrics or forms that should be available for students as the menus are introduced. If a menu has a free-choice option, the appropriate proposal form also will be listed here.

CHAPTER 5

Motion

20 Points
☐ _____
☐ _____
50 Points
☐ _____
☐ _____
☐ _____
☐ _____
80 Points
☐ _____
☐ _____

Significant Figures

20-50-80 Menu

Objectives Covered Through This Menu and These Activities

- Students will be able to explain and calculate significant figures accurately.
- Students will be able to state the importance of significant figures when completing calculations.

Materials Needed by Students for Completion

- Poster board or large white paper
- Large blank lined index cards (for instruction cards)
- Holiday lights (for quiz boards)
- Aluminum foil (for quiz boards)
- Wires (for quiz boards)
- Recording software or application (for videos)

Special Notes on the Use of This Menu

- This menu gives students the opportunity to create a video. The grading and sharing of these products can often be facilitated by having students prerecord their product using whatever technology is most convenient for the teacher. This allows the teacher to decide when it will be shown as well as keeps the presentation to its intended length. If recording options are limited, this activity can be modified by allowing students to act out the product (like a play) in front of the class.

Time Frame

- 1–2 weeks—Students are given a menu as the unit is started, and the teacher discusses all of the product options on the menu. As the different options are discussed, students will choose the activities they are most interested in completing so that they meet their goal of 100 points. As the lessons progress through the week(s), the teacher and students refer back to the menu options associated with the content being taught.
- 1–2 days—The teacher chooses an activity or product from the menu to use with the entire class.

Suggested Forms

- All-purpose rubric
- Proposal form for point-based projects

Name:_____ Date:_____

Significant Figures

Directions: Choose at least two activities from the menu below. The activities must total 100 points. Place a checkmark next to each box to show which activities you will complete. All activities must be completed by _____ .

20 Points

❐ Write an instruction card that tells the steps needed to determine the significant figures of a measurement.

❐ Design a folded quiz book with questions about numbers with 1–5 significant figures. Your questions should include a variety of examples that include zeros.

50 Points

❐ Write and perform an original song that could be used to help others understand how to give answers to word problems using the correct number of significant figures. Your song should include at least one example.

❐ Build a quiz board that requires matching word problems to answers with the number of significant figures. Each problem and answer should include at least one zero. Be tricky!

❐ Write Three Facts and a Fib about the common mistakes people make when determining the significant figures of a number.

❐ **Free choice on using significant figures**—Prepare a proposal form and submit it to your teacher for approval.

80 Points

❐ Record an instructional video on significant figures. Your video should include examples, how to calculate them, and why significant figures are important in physics calculations.

❐ Investigate the importance of accurate significant figures on research in the sciences. Write an essay that shares at least one occasion when a mistake in significant figures impacted a research project.

Motion Graphs

Tic-Tac-Toe Menu

Objectives Covered Through This Menu and These Activities

- Students will generate and interpret graphs and charts describing different types of motion, including displacement, velocity, and acceleration.
- Students will describe and analyze motion in one dimension with the concepts of distance, displacement, speed, and acceleration.
- Students will express, manipulate, and interpret relationships to make predictions and solve problems.
- Students will communicate valid conclusions supported by data or calculations.

Materials Needed by Students for Completion

- Poster board or large white paper
- Large blank lined index cards (for instruction cards)
- Blank index cards (for concentration cards)
- Scrapbooking materials (or electronic portfolio)

Special Notes on the Use of This Menu

- None

Time Frame

- 2–3 weeks—Students are given the menu as the unit is started. The teacher will go over all of the options for that content and have students place checkmarks in the boxes that represent the activities they are most interested in completing. As students choose activities, they should complete a column or a row. When students complete this pattern, they have completed one activity from each content area, learning style, or level of Bloom's revised taxonomy, depending on the design of the menu. As the teacher presents lessons throughout the week, they should refer back to the menu options associated with that content.
- 1 week—At the start of the unit, the teacher chooses the three activities they feel are most valuable for students. Stations can be set up in

the classroom. These three activities are available for student choice throughout the week as regular instruction takes place.

- 1–2 days—The teacher chooses an activity from the menu to use with the entire class.

Suggested Forms

- All-purpose rubric
- Free-choice proposal form

Motion Graphs

Directions: Check the boxes you plan to complete. They should form a tic-tac-toe across or down. All products are due by: _____ .

☐ *Displacement Versus Time* Write an instruction card that explains how to draw displacement versus time graphs with linear and parabolic shapes. Include a real-world example of each.	☐ *Acceleration Versus Time* Construct a set of concentration cards in which players match real-world events with acceleration versus time graphs that represent them.	☐ *Velocity Versus Time* On a poster, draw a velocity versus time graph for a car participating in the first three laps of the Indy 500. Use this graph to show how far the car traveled in those three laps.
☐ *Velocity Versus Time* Assemble a scrapbook of different events you experience daily that could be represented on a velocity versus time graph. Include a graph for each entry.	☐ **Free Choice: Displacement Versus Time** (Fill out your proposal form before beginning the free choice!)	☐ *Acceleration Versus Time* Determine the significance of the slope of an acceleration versus time graph. Write Three Facts and a Fib about this measurement using a real-world example.
☐ *Acceleration Versus Time* Some sources have called this motion graph "trivial." Prepare a social media profile for this graph, focusing on its importance when discussing motion.	☐ *Velocity Versus Time* Create one graph that could be a velocity versus time or displacement versus time graph depending on the labels of its axes. Write two paragraphs to share the story behind each possible graph.	☐ *Displacement Versus Time* Design a folded quiz book for displacement versus time graphs. Your questions should include positive, negative, and line of best fit graphs using real-world examples. (*Note:* Questions must be your original work.)

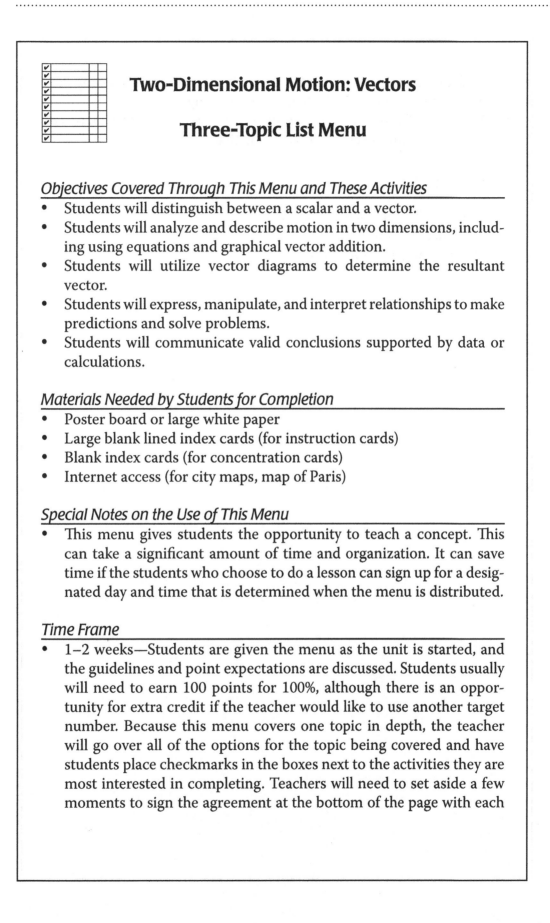

Two-Dimensional Motion: Vectors

Three-Topic List Menu

Objectives Covered Through This Menu and These Activities
- Students will distinguish between a scalar and a vector.
- Students will analyze and describe motion in two dimensions, including using equations and graphical vector addition.
- Students will utilize vector diagrams to determine the resultant vector.
- Students will express, manipulate, and interpret relationships to make predictions and solve problems.
- Students will communicate valid conclusions supported by data or calculations.

Materials Needed by Students for Completion
- Poster board or large white paper
- Large blank lined index cards (for instruction cards)
- Blank index cards (for concentration cards)
- Internet access (for city maps, map of Paris)

Special Notes on the Use of This Menu
- This menu gives students the opportunity to teach a concept. This can take a significant amount of time and organization. It can save time if the students who choose to do a lesson can sign up for a designated day and time that is determined when the menu is distributed.

Time Frame
- 1–2 weeks—Students are given the menu as the unit is started, and the guidelines and point expectations are discussed. Students usually will need to earn 100 points for 100%, although there is an opportunity for extra credit if the teacher would like to use another target number. Because this menu covers one topic in depth, the teacher will go over all of the options for the topic being covered and have students place checkmarks in the boxes next to the activities they are most interested in completing. Teachers will need to set aside a few moments to sign the agreement at the bottom of the page with each

student. As instruction continues, activities are completed by students and submitted to the teacher for grading.

- 1–2 days—The teacher chooses an activity or product from an objective to use with the entire class during that lesson time.

Suggested Forms

- All-purpose rubric
- Proposal form for point-based products
- Presentation rubric
- Student-taught lesson rubric

Name:_____ Date:_____

Two-Dimensional Motion: Vectors

Guidelines:

1. You may complete as many of the activities listed as you wish within the time period.
2. You may choose any combination of activities, but **must** complete at least one activity from each topic area.
3. Your goal is 100 points. (This is a grade of 100/100.) You may earn up to _____ points extra credit.
4. You may be as creative as you like within the guidelines listed below.
5. You must show your plan to your teacher by _____ .
6. Activities may be turned in at any time during the working time period. They will be graded and recorded on this sheet as you continue to work, so keep it safe!

Topic	Plan to Do	Activity to Complete	Point Value	Date Completed	Points Earned
Scalar and Vector		Write a T-Chart of measurements that are scalar and vector.	10		
		Make two acrostics, one for *scalar* and one for *vector*. Record appropriate scalar and vector measurements for each word.	15		
		Propose a class game in which participants compete to make or calculate real-world scalar and vector measurements.	20		
		Is it necessary to use vectors? Write a story in which scalar measurements are used rather than vector, causing confusion for the characters.	30		
Resultant Vectors		Write an instruction card that explains how to draw vectors and calculate resultant vectors.	15		
		Create a set of concentration cards in which players match situations with resultant vector drawings resulting from multiple vectors.	20		
		Using a map of a city with square blocks, create a worksheet for your classmates in which they calculate displacement using resultant vectors.	25		
		A tourist beginning at the Eiffel Tower wanted to visit the Louvre, Notre Dame, and the Arc de Triomphe. Using a map of Paris, prepare a poster with the best route that would cover the least distance and would leave them closest to their starting point.	30		
Calculations With Vectors		Design a flipbook for each type of vector calculation with an example of each.	10		
		Create a folded quiz book that could be used to review all of the vector calculations we have used in this unit.	15		
		Develop your own *original* real-world vector problem that requires solving for an angle to answer it.	20		
		Poll your classmates to discover which vector concepts and calculations are the most confusing. Prepare a student-taught lesson in which you share a different method of understanding the most confusing topics.	30		
Any		**Free Choice:** Submit your free-choice proposal form for a product of your choice.			
		Total number of points you are planning to earn.		**Total points earned:**	

I am planning to complete _____ activities that could earn up to a total of _____ points.

Teacher's initials _____ Student's signature _____

```
20 Points
□ _____
□ _____
50 Points
□ _____
□ _____
□ _____
□ _____
80 Points
□ _____
□ _____
```

Projectile Motion

20-50-80 Menu

Objectives Covered Through This Menu and These Activities

- Students will analyze and describe accelerated motion in two dimensions.
- Students will recognize that, when neglecting air resistance, a projectile has a constant horizontal velocity and a constant vertical free-fall acceleration.
- Students will identify and describe examples of projectile motion.

Materials Needed by Students for Completion

- Poster board or large white paper
- Blank index cards (for trading cards)
- Magazines (for collages, sports photos)
- Graph paper or Internet access (for WebQuests)
- Recycled materials (for trebuchet)

Special Notes on the Use of This Menu

- This menu asks students to use recycled materials to create their trebuchet. This does not mean only plastic and paper; instead, students should focus on using materials in new ways. It works well if a box is started for "recycled" contributions at the beginning of the school year. That way, students always have access to these types of materials.
- This menu allows students to create a WebQuest. There are multiple versions and templates for WebQuests available on the Internet. It is your decision whether you would like to specify a format or if you will allow students to create one of their own choosing.

Time Frame

- 1–2 weeks—Students are given a menu as the unit is started, and the teacher discusses all of the product options on the menu. As the different options are discussed, students will choose the activities they are most interested in completing so that they meet their goal of 100 points. As the lessons progress through the week(s), the teacher and students refer back to the menu options associated with the content being taught.

- 1–2 days—The teacher chooses an activity or product from the menu to use with the entire class.

Suggested Forms

- All-purpose rubric
- Proposal form for point-based projects
- Presentation rubric

Projectile Motion

Directions: Choose at least two activities from the menu below. The activities must total 100 points. Place a checkmark next to each box to show which activities you will complete. All activities must be completed by _____ .

20 Points

- ❒ Create a set of trading cards for different objects that demonstrate projectile motion. Be sure to include qualities that confirm each object has projectile motion.

- ❒ Write Three Facts and a Fib about objects that have projectile motion. Be sure your fib is tricky!

50 Points

- ❒ Draw a Venn diagram to compare projectile motion and parabolic calculations.

- ❒ Create a collage of at least five examples of projectile motion. Label each picture with realistic horizontal and vertical measurements. Create one original word problem to accompany one of the examples.

- ❒ Find a sports photo that represents projectile motion. Use your photo to write an original realistic word problem related to your photo. Your problem should include a diagram as well as the processes to solve the problem.

- ❒ **Free choice on analyzing projectile motion**—Prepare a proposal form and submit it to your teacher for approval.

80 Points

- ❒ Design a WebQuest in which questors visit different websites to experience how different factors impact the motion of real-world projectiles.

- ❒ Construct a trebuchet that weighs less than 100 g that can send a projectile at least 4 m. Record a video or create a poster to share how your model was constructed and tests performed to confirm its success.

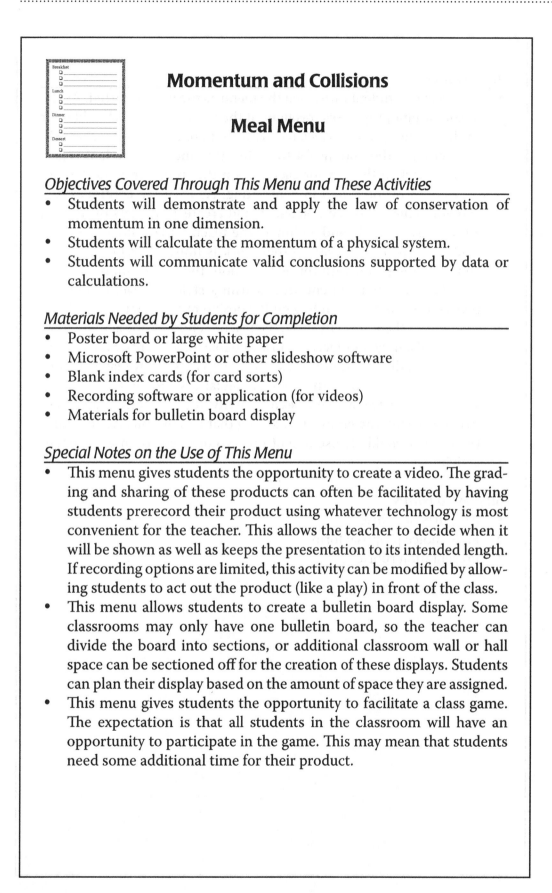

Momentum and Collisions

Meal Menu

Objectives Covered Through This Menu and These Activities

- Students will demonstrate and apply the law of conservation of momentum in one dimension.
- Students will calculate the momentum of a physical system.
- Students will communicate valid conclusions supported by data or calculations.

Materials Needed by Students for Completion

- Poster board or large white paper
- Microsoft PowerPoint or other slideshow software
- Blank index cards (for card sorts)
- Recording software or application (for videos)
- Materials for bulletin board display

Special Notes on the Use of This Menu

- This menu gives students the opportunity to create a video. The grading and sharing of these products can often be facilitated by having students prerecord their product using whatever technology is most convenient for the teacher. This allows the teacher to decide when it will be shown as well as keeps the presentation to its intended length. If recording options are limited, this activity can be modified by allowing students to act out the product (like a play) in front of the class.
- This menu allows students to create a bulletin board display. Some classrooms may only have one bulletin board, so the teacher can divide the board into sections, or additional classroom wall or hall space can be sectioned off for the creation of these displays. Students can plan their display based on the amount of space they are assigned.
- This menu gives students the opportunity to facilitate a class game. The expectation is that all students in the classroom will have an opportunity to participate in the game. This may mean that students need some additional time for their product.

Time Frame

- 2–3 weeks—Students are given the menu as the unit is started. As the lesson or unit progresses throughout the week, students should refer to the menu options associated with that content. The teacher will go over all of the options for that objective and have students place a checkmark in the box for each option that represents the activity they are most interested in completing. As teaching continues, the activities chosen and completed should create a full day's meal, with a breakfast, a lunch, and a dinner. The teacher may choose to allow students time to work after other work is finished. When students complete the menu with this expectation, they have completed one activity from each content area, learning style, or level of Bloom's revised taxonomy, depending on the design of the menu.
- 1 week—At the start of the unit, the teacher chooses one activity from each meal family they feel are most valuable for students. Stations can be set up in the classroom. These three activities are available for student choice throughout the week as regular instruction takes place.
- 1–2 days—The teacher chooses an activity or product from an objective to use with the entire class during that lesson time. Additionally, the teacher could choose one of the two desserts as an enrichment activity.

Suggested Forms

- All-purpose rubric
- Free-choice proposal form
- Presentation rubric

Name:_____ Date:_____

Momentum and Collisions

Directions: Choose an activity from each meal below. You must complete these activities in order, progressing from breakfast, to lunch, and then dinner. Place a checkmark next to each box to show which activities you will complete. All activities must be completed by: _____ .

Breakfast

☐ Design a social media profile for the law of conservation of momentum. Have fun with its relationships and interactions with its "friends."

☐ Prepare a stand-alone PowerPoint presentation with examples of momentum, impulse, and factors that affect each value.

☐ Write a folded quiz book about the law of conservation of momentum in our daily lives.

Lunch

☐ Create a card sort in which players will sort descriptions of interactions between a variety of objects by the type of collision represented.

☐ Record a video in the style of Steve Irwin in which you investigate different (safe!) momentum collisions.

☐ Develop a bulletin board display that uses famous sports moments to demonstrate different types of momentum collisions. Be sure to include the forces in each example.

Dinner

☐ Write a choose-your-own-adventure story in which readers must solve and find errors in different collision problems to make choices in the story.

☐ Invent a class game for your classmates to hone their skills in modeling and solving momentum experiences.

☐ **Free choice on momentum's impact on our daily lives (with calculations)—** Prepare a proposal form and submit it to your teacher for approval.

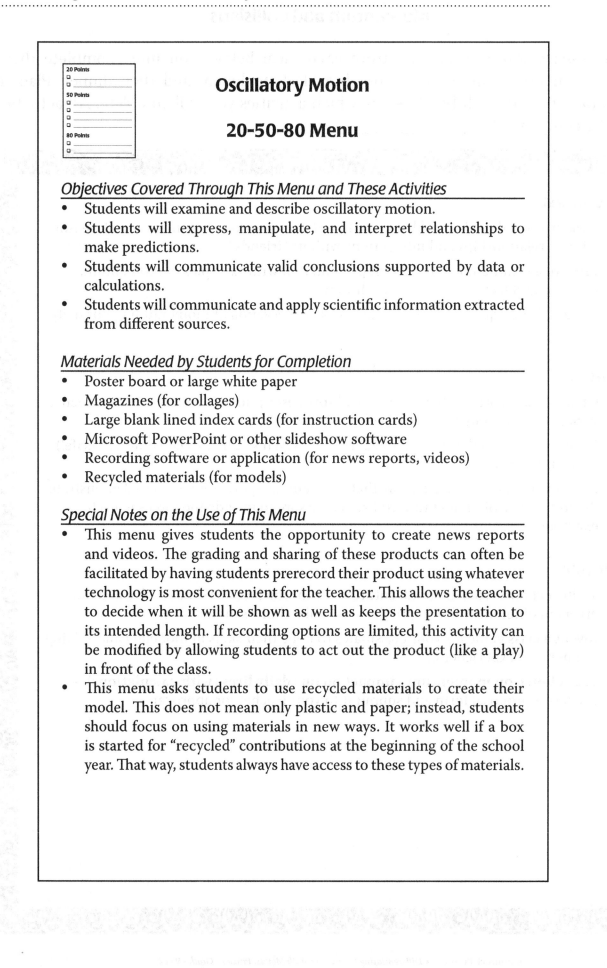

20 Points
☐ _____
☐ _____
50 Points
☐ _____
☐ _____
☐ _____
80 Points
☐ _____
☐ _____

Oscillatory Motion

20-50-80 Menu

Objectives Covered Through This Menu and These Activities
- Students will examine and describe oscillatory motion.
- Students will express, manipulate, and interpret relationships to make predictions.
- Students will communicate valid conclusions supported by data or calculations.
- Students will communicate and apply scientific information extracted from different sources.

Materials Needed by Students for Completion
- Poster board or large white paper
- Magazines (for collages)
- Large blank lined index cards (for instruction cards)
- Microsoft PowerPoint or other slideshow software
- Recording software or application (for news reports, videos)
- Recycled materials (for models)

Special Notes on the Use of This Menu
- This menu gives students the opportunity to create news reports and videos. The grading and sharing of these products can often be facilitated by having students prerecord their product using whatever technology is most convenient for the teacher. This allows the teacher to decide when it will be shown as well as keeps the presentation to its intended length. If recording options are limited, this activity can be modified by allowing students to act out the product (like a play) in front of the class.
- This menu asks students to use recycled materials to create their model. This does not mean only plastic and paper; instead, students should focus on using materials in new ways. It works well if a box is started for "recycled" contributions at the beginning of the school year. That way, students always have access to these types of materials.

Time Frame

- 1–2 weeks—Students are given a menu as the unit is started, and the teacher discusses all of the product options on the menu. As the different options are discussed, students will choose the activities they are most interested in completing so that they meet their goal of 100 points. As the lessons progress through the week(s), the teacher and students refer back to the menu options associated with the content being taught.
- 1–2 days—The teacher chooses an activity or product from the menu to use with the entire class.

Suggested Forms

- All-purpose rubric
- Proposal form for point-based projects
- Presentation rubric

Oscillatory Motion

Directions: Choose at least two activities from the menu below. The activities must total 100 points. Place a checkmark next to each box to show which activities you will complete. All activities must be completed by _____ .

---

20 Points

- ❏ Create a poster to show the movement of a pendulum and its different measurements.

- ❏ Assemble a collage of different types of pendulums. Label important measurements on each.

---

50 Points

- ❏ If a grandfather clock is running too fast or too slow, the time will be incorrect. Write an instruction card to explain how to make the clock run correctly. Include an illustration for and the reasoning behind each step.

- ❏ Playground swings can be considered pendulums. Prepare a PowerPoint presentation that teaches others about the physics behind swing set design that allows the swing to work, while keeping the child swinging safe.

- ❏ Wrecking balls are large pendulums. Record a news report about a surprising incident in which you provide physics explanations for why a wrecking ball did not perform as expected.

- ❏ **Free choice on oscillatory motion in the world around us**—Prepare a proposal form and submit it to your teacher for approval.

---

80 Points

- ❏ Build a model of a pendulum that has a period of 1.5 s. Be prepared to demonstrate your pendulum and include calculations with instructions for constructing your model.

- ❏ Research large pendulums (often found in museums) that can be used to tell the time. Record a video that shares the physics behind these large timepieces.

CHAPTER 6

Forces

20 Points
☐ _____
☐ _____
50 Points
☐ _____
☐ _____
☐ _____
☐ _____
80 Points
☐ _____
☐ _____

Free Body Diagrams

20-50-80 Menu

Objectives Covered Through This Menu and These Activities

- Students will be able to draw and interpret force when shown free body diagrams.
- Students will express, manipulate, and interpret relationships to make predictions and solve problems.
- Students will communicate valid conclusions supported by data or calculations.

Materials Needed by Students for Completion

- Poster board or large white paper
- Large blank lined index cards (for instruction cards)
- Recycled materials (for models)
- Blank index cards (for concentration cards)
- Scrapbooking materials (or electronic portfolios)
- Recording software or application (for videos)

Special Notes on the Use of This Menu

- This menu gives students the opportunity to create a video. The grading and sharing of these products can often be facilitated by having students prerecord their product using whatever technology is most convenient for the teacher. This allows the teacher to decide when it will be shown as well as keeps the presentation to its intended length. If recording options are limited, this activity can be modified by allowing students to act out the product (like a play) in front of the class.
- This menu asks students to use recycled materials to create their model. This does not mean only plastic and paper; instead, students should focus on using materials in new ways. It works well if a box is started for "recycled" contributions at the beginning of the school year. That way, students always have access to these types of materials.
- This menu gives students the opportunity to present information about a rollercoaster. This can take a significant amount of time and organization. It can save time if the demonstration is prerecorded (using whatever technology is most convenient) to share at a later time, or if the teacher prefers "live" demonstrations, all of the stu-

dents who choose to do a demonstration can sign up for a designated day and time that is determined when the menu is distributed.

Time Frame

- 1–2 weeks—Students are given a menu as the unit is started, and the teacher discusses all of the product options on the menu. As the different options are discussed, students will choose the activities they are most interested in completing so that they meet their goal of 100 points. As the lessons progress through the week(s), the teacher and students refer back to the menu options associated with the content being taught.
- 1–2 days—The teacher chooses an activity or product from the menu to use with the entire class.

Suggested Forms

- All-purpose rubric
- Proposal form for point-based projects
- Presentation rubric

Free Body Diagrams

Directions: Choose at least two activities from the menu below. The activities must total 100 points. Place a checkmark next to each box to show which activities you will complete. All activities must be completed by _____ .

20 Points

❏ Write an instruction card that explains how to draw and label all forces on a free body diagram.

❏ Make a model of a free body diagram with all forces labeled.

50 Points

❏ Select an action scene from an action movie or video. On a poster, draw a free body diagram to show realistic forces at work on the person or object from the video.

❏ Create a set of concentration cards in which users match unique real-world descriptions (including data) with different free body diagrams.

❏ Design a scrapbook of nature photos with a corresponding free body diagram on each.

❏ **Free choice on free body diagrams**—Prepare a proposal form and submit it to your teacher for approval.

80 Points

❏ Choose a roller coaster from a popular theme park. Research the rollercoaster's path and create a presentation that shares information about the rollercoaster and at least eight free body diagrams along the path of rollercoaster's path.

❏ Based on Newton's third law of motion, every action has an equal and opposite reaction. Is this also true for forces in the world around us? Record a video in which you consider this idea and use free body diagrams of everyday occurrences to investigate your hypothesis.

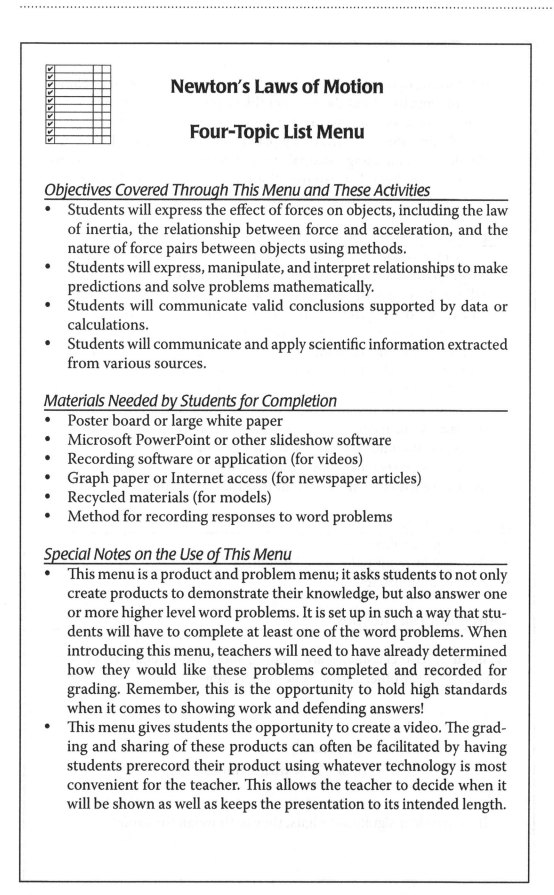

Newton's Laws of Motion

Four-Topic List Menu

Objectives Covered Through This Menu and These Activities
- Students will express the effect of forces on objects, including the law of inertia, the relationship between force and acceleration, and the nature of force pairs between objects using methods.
- Students will express, manipulate, and interpret relationships to make predictions and solve problems mathematically.
- Students will communicate valid conclusions supported by data or calculations.
- Students will communicate and apply scientific information extracted from various sources.

Materials Needed by Students for Completion
- Poster board or large white paper
- Microsoft PowerPoint or other slideshow software
- Recording software or application (for videos)
- Graph paper or Internet access (for newspaper articles)
- Recycled materials (for models)
- Method for recording responses to word problems

Special Notes on the Use of This Menu
- This menu is a product and problem menu; it asks students to not only create products to demonstrate their knowledge, but also answer one or more higher level word problems. It is set up in such a way that students will have to complete at least one of the word problems. When introducing this menu, teachers will need to have already determined how they would like these problems completed and recorded for grading. Remember, this is the opportunity to hold high standards when it comes to showing work and defending answers!
- This menu gives students the opportunity to create a video. The grading and sharing of these products can often be facilitated by having students prerecord their product using whatever technology is most convenient for the teacher. This allows the teacher to decide when it will be shown as well as keeps the presentation to its intended length.

If recording options are limited, this activity can be modified by allowing students to act out the product (like a play) in front of the class.
- This menu asks students to use recycled materials to create their model. This does not mean only plastic and paper; instead, students should focus on using materials in new ways. It works well if a box is started for "recycled" contributions at the beginning of the school year. That way, students always have access to these types of materials.

Time Frame

- 1–2 weeks—Students are given the menu as the unit is started, and the guidelines and point expectations are discussed. Students usually will need to earn 100 points for 100%, although there is an opportunity for extra credit if the teacher would like to use another target number. Because this menu covers one topic in depth, the teacher will go over all of the options for the topic being covered and have students place checkmarks in the boxes next to the activities they are most interested in completing. Teachers will need to set aside a few moments to sign the agreement at the bottom of the page with each student. As instruction continues, activities are completed by students and submitted to the teacher for grading.
- 1–2 days—The teacher chooses an activity or product from an objective to use with the entire class during that lesson time.

Suggested Forms

- All-purpose rubric
- Proposal form for point-based products
- Presentation rubric

Answers to Menu Problems

Problem 1: Two classmates are arguing about who weighs more. One weighs 72 kg, the other 710 N. Who weighs more?

$$F = ma$$
$$F = 72 \text{ kg}(9.8 \text{ m/s}^2)$$
$$F = 705.6 \text{ or } 710 \text{ N with significant digits}$$

If we consider significant digits, they both weigh the same.

Problem 2: Five students are pushing a homecoming float. Each person has a mass of approximately 62 kg and pushes with a 321 N force. What is the mass of the float if it accelerates at 0.72 m/s²?

$$F = ma$$
$$F = (5 \text{ people})(321 \text{ N})$$
$$F = 1605 \text{ N}$$

$$F = ma$$
$$\frac{1605 \text{ N}}{.72 \text{ m/s}^2} = \frac{m(.72 \text{ m/s}^2)}{.72 \text{ m/s}^2}$$
$$2{,}229 \text{ kg} = m$$

The float has a mass of 2,200 kg.

Problem 3: A new sports car can accelerate from 0 to 70 mph (31 m/s), in 7.4 s. What is the mass of the car if the force exerted by the car is 4,106 N?

$$A = \frac{v_f - v_i}{t}$$
$$A = \frac{31 \text{ m/s} - 0 \text{ m/s}}{7.4 \text{ s}}$$
$$A = 4.2 \text{ m/s}^2$$
$$F = ma$$
$$\frac{4{,}106 \text{ N}}{4.2 \text{ m/s}^2} = \frac{m(4.2 \text{ m/s}^2)}{4.2 \text{ m/s}^2}$$
$$978 \text{ kg} = m$$

The mass is 978 kg.

Problem 4: A speedboat and its captain with a mass of 734 kg have an acceleration of 0.723 m/s². If a competitor wanted to sabotage the speedboat so it could not accelerate more than 0.530 m/s², how much weight would they have to add to the bottom of the boat?

$$F = ma$$
$$F = (743 \text{ kg})(.723 \text{ m/s}^2)$$
$$F = 537 \text{ N}$$

$$F = ma$$
$$\frac{537 \text{ N}}{.530 \text{ m/s}^2} = \frac{m(.530 \text{ m/s}^2)}{.530 \text{ m/s}^2}$$
$$1{,}013.2 \text{ kg} = m$$
$$1{,}010 \text{ kg} = m$$
$$1{,}010 \text{ kg} - 734 \text{ kg} = 276 \text{ kg}$$

They would need to add 276 kg.

Name:_____ Date:_____

Newton's Laws of Motion

Guidelines:

1. You may complete as many of the activities listed as you wish within the time period.
2. You may choose any combination of activities, but **must** complete at least one activity from each topic area.
3. Your goal is 125 points. (This is a grade of 100/100.) You may earn up to _____ points extra credit.
4. You may be as creative as you like within the guidelines listed below.
5. You must show your plan to your teacher by _____ .
6. Activities may be turned in at any time during the working time period. They will be graded and recorded on this sheet as you continue to work, so keep it safe!

Topic	Plan to Do	Activity to Complete	Point Value	Date Completed	Points Earned
Newton's First Law		Make an acrostic for the word *inertia*. Provide examples of inertia for each letter.	10		
		Prepare a PowerPoint presentation that shares different examples of Newton's first law of motion in the world around us.	15		
		Find a newspaper article with an example of Newton's first law of motion. Make a poster to share your article and how it contains an appropriate example.	20		
		Record a video to show inertia at work in the sports people play.	25		
Newton's Second Law		Make a windowpane for the variables in the formula associated with Newton's second law of motion. Include the equation solved for each variable.	10		
		Build a model that could be used to demonstrate Newton's second law of motion.	15		
		Draw a Venn diagram to compare Newton's first and second laws of motion.	20		
		Keep a dairy or journal for 2 days in which your record all of your experiences with Newton's second law of motion.	25		
Newton's Third Law		Write Three Facts and a Fib about Newton's third law of motion.	15		
		Design a worksheet with *original* word problems to test your classmates' skills over Newton's third law of motion.	20		
		It has been proposed that any motion can be explained by all three of Newton's laws of motion. Prepare a product that shows that is this idea is true.	25		
		A new award has been made to acknowledge the best use of Newton's third law of motion last year. Decide who should earn the award and write their acceptance speech detailing their efforts.	30		

Name:_____ Date:_____

Newton's Laws of Motion, continued

Topic	Plan to Do	Activity to Complete	Point Value	Date Completed	Points Earned
Real-World Problems		**Problem 1:** Two classmates are arguing about who weighs more. One weighs 72 kg, the other 710 N. Who weighs more?	15		
		Problem 2: Five students are pushing a homecoming float. Each person has a mass of approximately 62 kg and pushes with a 321 N force. What is the mass of the float if it accelerates at 0.72 m/s²?	20		
		Problem 3: A new sports car can accelerate from 0 to 70 mph (31 m/s), in 7.4 s. What is the mass of the car if the force exerted by the car is 4,106 N?	25		
		Problem 4: A speedboat and its captain with a mass of 734 kg have an acceleration of 0.723 m/s². If a competitor wanted to sabotage the speedboat so it could not accelerate more than 0.530 m/s², how much weight would they have to add to the bottom of the boat?	25		
Any		**Free Choice:** Submit your free-choice proposal form for a product of your choice.			
		Total number of points you are planning to earn.		Total points earned:	

I am planning to complete _____ activities that could earn up to a total of _____ points.

Teacher's initials _____ Student's signature _____

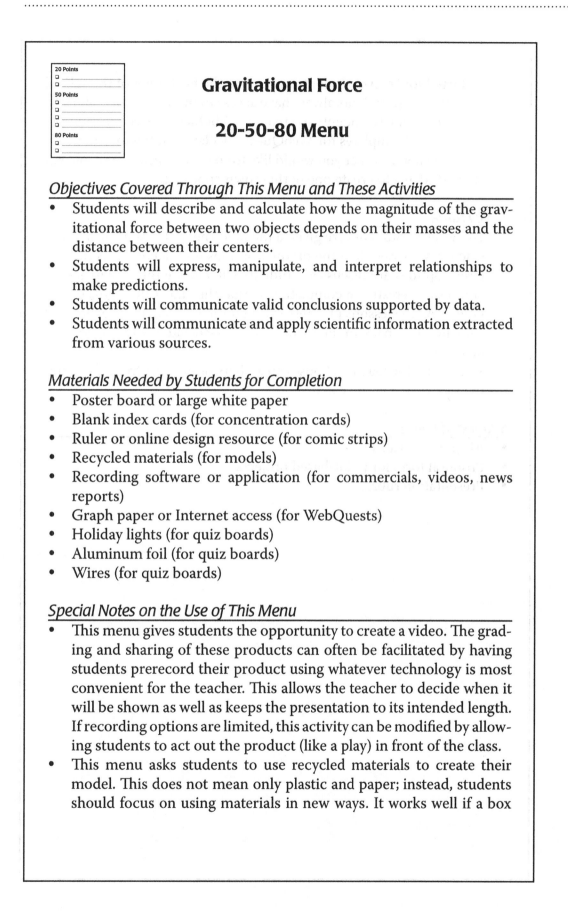

Gravitational Force

20-50-80 Menu

20 Points

☐ _____
☐ _____

50 Points

☐ _____
☐ _____
☐ _____

80 Points

☐ _____
☐ _____

Objectives Covered Through This Menu and These Activities

- Students will describe and calculate how the magnitude of the gravitational force between two objects depends on their masses and the distance between their centers.
- Students will express, manipulate, and interpret relationships to make predictions.
- Students will communicate valid conclusions supported by data.
- Students will communicate and apply scientific information extracted from various sources.

Materials Needed by Students for Completion

- Poster board or large white paper
- Blank index cards (for concentration cards)
- Ruler or online design resource (for comic strips)
- Recycled materials (for models)
- Recording software or application (for commercials, videos, news reports)
- Graph paper or Internet access (for WebQuests)
- Holiday lights (for quiz boards)
- Aluminum foil (for quiz boards)
- Wires (for quiz boards)

Special Notes on the Use of This Menu

- This menu gives students the opportunity to create a video. The grading and sharing of these products can often be facilitated by having students prerecord their product using whatever technology is most convenient for the teacher. This allows the teacher to decide when it will be shown as well as keeps the presentation to its intended length. If recording options are limited, this activity can be modified by allowing students to act out the product (like a play) in front of the class.
- This menu asks students to use recycled materials to create their model. This does not mean only plastic and paper; instead, students should focus on using materials in new ways. It works well if a box

is started for "recycled" contributions at the beginning of the school year. That way, students always have access to these types of materials.

- This menu allows students to create a WebQuest. There are multiple versions and templates for WebQuests available on the Internet. It is your decision whether you would like to specify a format or if you will allow students to create one of their own choosing.

Time Frame

- 1–2 weeks—Students are given a menu as the unit is started, and the teacher discusses all of the product options on the menu. As the different options are discussed, students will choose the activities they are most interested in completing so that they meet their goal of 100 points. As the lessons progress through the week(s), the teacher and students refer back to the menu options associated with the content being taught.
- 1–2 days—The teacher chooses an activity or product from the menu to use with the entire class.

Suggested Forms

- All-purpose rubric
- Proposal form for point-based projects
- Presentation rubric

Gravitational Force

Directions: Choose at least two activities from the menu below. The activities must total 100 points. Place a checkmark next to each box to show which activities you will complete. All activities must be completed by _____ .

---

20 Points

❒ Write Three Facts and a Fib about gravitational forces and their impact on the properties of everyday objects.

❒ Create a set of concentration cards to match gravitational force word problems with the correct setup to solve each problem.

---

50 Points

❒ Design a quiz board in which players match original real-world gravitational problems with setups and answers.

❒ Draw a comic strip in which a "large-bodied" superhero uses their powers to defeat an enemy through gravitational force.

❒ Build a model that could be used to demonstrate how the gravitational force between two objects can change. Be sure to include calculations to support your model.

❒ **Free choice on gravitational force**—Prepare a proposal form and submit it to your teacher for approval.

---

80 Points

❒ Some science fiction movies are based on real science; others are not. Record a sci-fi documentary video about a planetary system like ours, but the system has another sun at Pluto's distance from Earth. Your film should explore gravitational calculations and how this sun's gravitational force will impact this system's Earth and the other planets.

❒ Prepare a WebQuest in which questors research different real-world situations to make predictions on the outcome of an event based on gravitational force calculations.

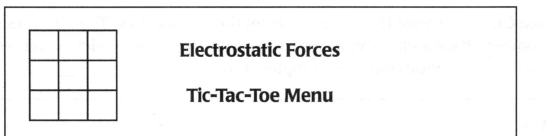

Electrostatic Forces

Tic-Tac-Toe Menu

Objectives Covered Through This Menu and These Activities

- Students will investigate electrostatic forces.
- Students will use Coulomb's law to determine electrostatic forces.
- Students will express, manipulate, and interpret relationships to make predictions and solve problems mathematically.
- Students will communicate valid conclusions supported by data or calculations.

Materials Needed by Students for Completion

- Poster board or large white paper
- Large blank lined index cards (for instruction cards)
- Ruler or online design resource (for comic strips)
- Blank index cards (for card sorts)
- Method for recording responses to word problems

Special Notes on the Use of This Menu

- This menu is a product and problem menu; it asks students to not only create products to demonstrate their knowledge, but also answer one or more higher level word problems. It is set up in such a way that students will have to complete at least one of the word problems. When introducing this menu, teachers will need to have already determined how they would like these problems completed and recorded for grading. Remember, this is the opportunity to hold high standards when it comes to showing work and defending answers!
- This menu gives students the opportunity to facilitate a class model. The expectation is that all students in the classroom will play an active role in the model. This may mean that students need some additional space for their model.

Time Frame

- 2–3 weeks—Students are given the menu as the unit is started. The teacher will go over all of the options for that content and have students place checkmarks in the boxes that represent the activities they are most interested in completing. As students choose activities, they should complete a column or a row. When students complete this pattern, they have completed one activity from each content area, learning style, or level of Bloom's revised taxonomy, depending on the design of the menu. As the teacher presents lessons throughout the week, they should refer back to the menu options associated with that content.

- 1 week—At the start of the unit, the teacher chooses the three activities they feel are most valuable for students. Stations can be set up in the classroom. These three activities are available for student choice throughout the week as regular instruction takes place.
- 1–2 days—The teacher chooses an activity from the menu to use with the entire class.

Suggested Forms

- All-purpose rubric
- Free-choice proposal form
- Presentation rubric

Answers to Menu Problems

Problem 1: A person gets out of a car, accumulating a charge of +3.1 × 10⁻⁵ C. The other person leaves the car with a charge of -7.6 × 10⁻⁵ C. What is the magnitude of the electrical force being exerted on each other if they are 7 m from each other?

$$F = k \cdot \frac{q_1 q_2}{d^2}$$

$$k = 9.0 \times 10^9 \frac{Nm^2}{C^2}$$

$$F = 9.0 \times 10^9 \frac{Nm^2}{C^2} \left(\frac{(+3.1 \times 10^{-5}C)(-7.0 \times 10^{-5}C)}{(7\,m)^2} \right)$$

$$F = 9.0 \times 10^9 \frac{Nm^2}{C^2} \left(\frac{-2.36 \times 10^{-9}C^2}{49\,m^2} \right)$$

$$F = \frac{-21.2\,Nm^2}{49\,m^2}$$

$$F = .43\,N$$

The force is .43 N.

Problem 2: A dancer accumulates a charge of 4.5×10^{-5} C. Another dancer accumulates a charge of -3.2×10^{-5} C. If the magnitude of the electrical force being exerted on each other is 32 N, how far apart are the dancers?

$$F = k\frac{q_1 q_2}{d^2}$$

$$d = \sqrt{\frac{k(q_1 q_2)}{F}}$$

$$d = \sqrt{\frac{9.0 \times 10^9 \frac{Nm^2}{C^2}(4.5 \times 10^{-5}C)(-3.2 \times 10^{-4}C)}{32\,N}}$$

$$d = \sqrt{\frac{12.96\,Nm^2}{32\,N}}$$

$$d = \sqrt{.405\,m}$$

$$d = .64\,m$$

They are .64 m or 64 cm away from each other.

Problem 3: A child runs on a rug, accumulating a charge of -2.3×10^{-5} C. Another child who is 3.7 m away is exerting an attractive force with a magnitude of .29 N on the first child. What is the second child's charge?

$$F = k\frac{q_1 q_2}{d^2}$$

$$q_2 = \frac{Fd^2}{kq_1}$$

$$q_2 = \frac{(.29\,N)(3.7\,m)^2}{(9.0 \times 10^9 \frac{Nm^2}{C^2})(-2.3 \times 10^{-5}C)}$$

$$q_2 = \frac{4.0\,Nm^2}{2.07 \times 10^5 \frac{Nm^2}{C^2}}$$

$$q_2 = 1.92 \times 10^{-5}C$$

The child's charge was 1.92×10^{-5} C.

Electrostatic Forces

Directions: Check the boxes you plan to complete. They should form a tic-tac-toe across or down. All products are due by: _____ .

☐ *Coulomb's Law* Research the history and development of Coulomb's law. Create an instruction card that explains different ways to use the law.	☐ *Problem 1* A person gets out of a car, accumulating a charge of $+3.1 \times 10^{-5}$ C. The other person leaves the car with a charge of -7.6×10^{-5} C. What is the magnitude of the electrical force being exerted on each other if they are 7 m from each other?	☐ *Conceptual Considerations* Propose a class model that could be used to demonstrate electrostatic forces on two different objects. Use your model to show how distance and charges impact the force.
☐ *Conceptual Considerations* Draw a comic strip about two particles who, although they cannot change their charges, change other aspects so they can be more attracted to each other.	☐ **Free Choice: Coulomb's Law** (Fill out your proposal form before beginning the free choice!)	☐ *Problem 2* A dancer accumulates a charge of 4.5×10^{-5} C. Another dancer accumulates a charge of -3.2×10^{-5} C. If the magnitude of the electrical force being exerted on each other is 32 N, how far apart are the dancers?
☐ *Problem 3* A child runs on a rug, accumulating a charge of -2.3×10^{-5} C. Another child who is 3.7 m away is exerting an attractive force with a magnitude of .29 N on the first child. What is the second child's charge?	☐ *Conceptual Considerations* Develop a card sort in which players match changing electrostatic force situations with the impact of the change. No calculations should be necessary.	☐ *Coulomb's Law* Create Three Facts and a Fib about values that can and cannot be calculated using Coulomb's law.

20 Points
☐ _____
☐ _____
50 Points
☐ _____
☐ _____
☐ _____
☐ _____
80 Points
☐ _____
☐ _____

Electric Conductors and Insulators

20-50-80 Menu

Objectives Covered Through This Menu and These Activities

- Students will characterize materials as conductors or insulators based on their electric properties.
- Students will communicate and apply scientific information extracted from various sources.
- Students will critique scientific explanations and evaluate the impact of research on scientific thought.

Materials Needed by Students for Completion

- Poster board or large white paper
- Blank index cards (for trading cards)
- Recycled materials (for models)
- Recording software or application (for videos)

Special Notes on the Use of This Menu

- This menu gives students the opportunity to create a video. The grading and sharing of these products can often be facilitated by having students prerecord their product using whatever technology is most convenient for the teacher. This allows the teacher to decide when it will be shown as well as keeps the presentation to its intended length. If recording options are limited, this activity can be modified by allowing students to act out the product (like a play) in front of the class.
- This menu asks students to use recycled materials to create their model. This does not mean only plastic and paper; instead, students should focus on using materials in new ways. It works well if a box is started for "recycled" contributions at the beginning of the school year. That way, students always have access to these types of materials.
- This menu gives students the opportunity to facilitate a class model. The expectation is that all students in the classroom will play an active role in the model. This may mean that students need some additional space for their model.

Time Frame

- 1–2 weeks—Students are given a menu as the unit is started, and the teacher discusses all of the product options on the menu. As the different options are discussed, students will choose the activities they are most interested in completing so that they meet their goal of 100 points. As the lessons progress through the week(s), the teacher and students refer back to the menu options associated with the content being taught.
- 1–2 days—The teacher chooses an activity or product from the menu to use with the entire class.

Suggested Forms

- All-purpose rubric
- Proposal form for point-based projects
- Presentation rubric

Electric Conductors and Insulators

Directions: Choose at least two activities from the menu below. The activities must total 100 points. Place a checkmark next to each box to show which activities you will complete. All activities must be completed by _____ .

---

20 Points

❑ Assemble a set of trading cards for everyday items that represent conductors and insulators. Include information about their properties on each.

❑ Build a model that shows the physical properties of electric conductors and insulators.

---

50 Points

❑ Research semiconductors and their use in electronics. Write an essay on their unique physical properties that make them valuable in industry.

❑ Design a social media profile for an electric conductor. Be creative!

❑ Brainstorm a classroom model to demonstrate the physical properties of conductors and insulators.

❑ **Free choice on electric insulators and conductors**—Prepare a proposal form and submit it to your teacher for approval.

---

80 Points

❑ Consider a substance that is an effective electric insulator. Without changing its chemical composition, record a video in which you propose three changes to the insulator to make it a conductor.

❑ You are working as an engineer for a space-based company. You have been asked to create a device that could be used to find electric conductors and insulators on other planets. You have been informed that you cannot use a battery or other energy source in its creation because of the length of the space flight. Prepare a poster to share your device and how it will function.

Electric Circuits

Tic-Tac-Toe Menu

Objectives Covered Through This Menu and These Activities
- Students will investigate and calculate current through, potential difference across, resistance of, and power used by electric circuit elements connected in both series and parallel combinations.
- Students will express, manipulate, and interpret relationships to make predictions and solve problems mathematically.
- Students will communicate valid conclusions supported by data or calculations.

Materials Needed by Students for Completion
- Poster board or large white paper
- Recording software or application (for videos)
- Microsoft PowerPoint or other slideshow software
- Method for writing situational problems

Special Notes on the Use of This Menu
- This menu gives students the opportunity to create a video. The grading and sharing of these products can often be facilitated by having students prerecord their product using whatever technology is most convenient for the teacher. This allows the teacher to decide when it will be shown as well as keeps the presentation to its intended length. If recording options are limited, this activity can be modified by allowing students to act out the product (like a play) in front of the class.

Time Frame
- 2–3 weeks—Students are given the menu as the unit is started. The teacher will go over all of the options for that content and have students place checkmarks in the boxes that represent the activities they are most interested in completing. As students choose activities, they should complete a column or a row. When students complete this pattern, they have completed one activity from each content area, learning style, or level of Bloom's revised taxonomy, depending on the design of the menu. As the teacher presents lessons throughout

the week, they should refer back to the menu options associated with that content.

- 1 week—At the start of the unit, the teacher chooses the three activities they feel are most valuable for students. Stations can be set up in the classroom. These three activities are available for student choice throughout the week as regular instruction takes place.
- 1–2 days—The teacher chooses an activity from the menu to use with the entire class.

Suggested Forms

- All-purpose rubric
- Free-choice proposal form
- Presentation rubric

Electric Circuits

Directions: Check the boxes you plan to complete. They should form a tic-tac-toe across or down. All products are due by: _____ .

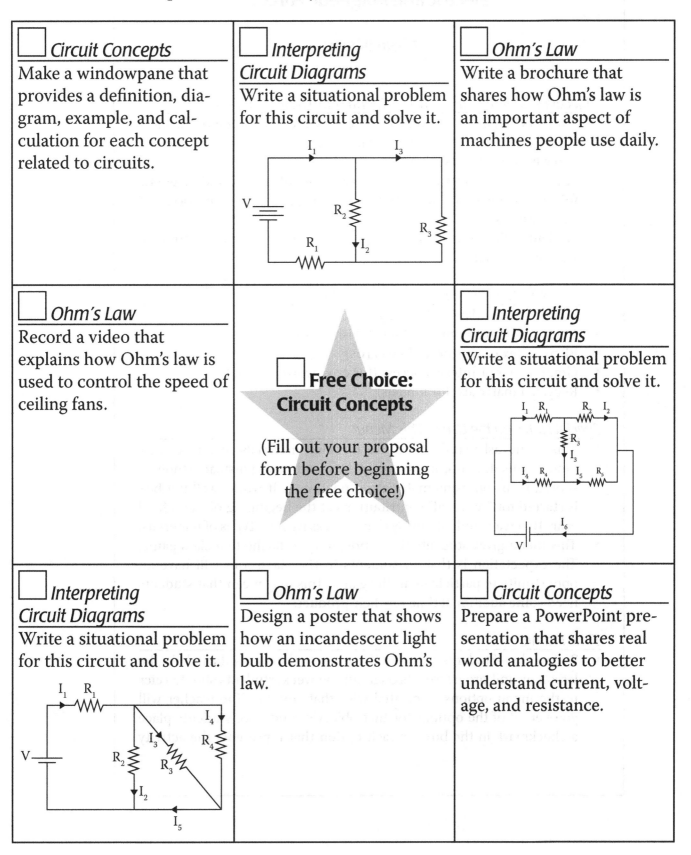

☐ *Circuit Concepts* Make a windowpane that provides a definition, diagram, example, and calculation for each concept related to circuits.	☐ *Interpreting Circuit Diagrams* Write a situational problem for this circuit and solve it.	☐ *Ohm's Law* Write a brochure that shares how Ohm's law is an important aspect of machines people use daily.
☐ *Ohm's Law* Record a video that explains how Ohm's law is used to control the speed of ceiling fans.	☐ **Free Choice:** **Circuit Concepts** (Fill out your proposal form before beginning the free choice!)	☐ *Interpreting Circuit Diagrams* Write a situational problem for this circuit and solve it.
☐ *Interpreting Circuit Diagrams* Write a situational problem for this circuit and solve it.	☐ *Ohm's Law* Design a poster that shows how an incandescent light bulb demonstrates Ohm's law.	☐ *Circuit Concepts* Prepare a PowerPoint presentation that shares real world analogies to better understand current, voltage, and resistance.

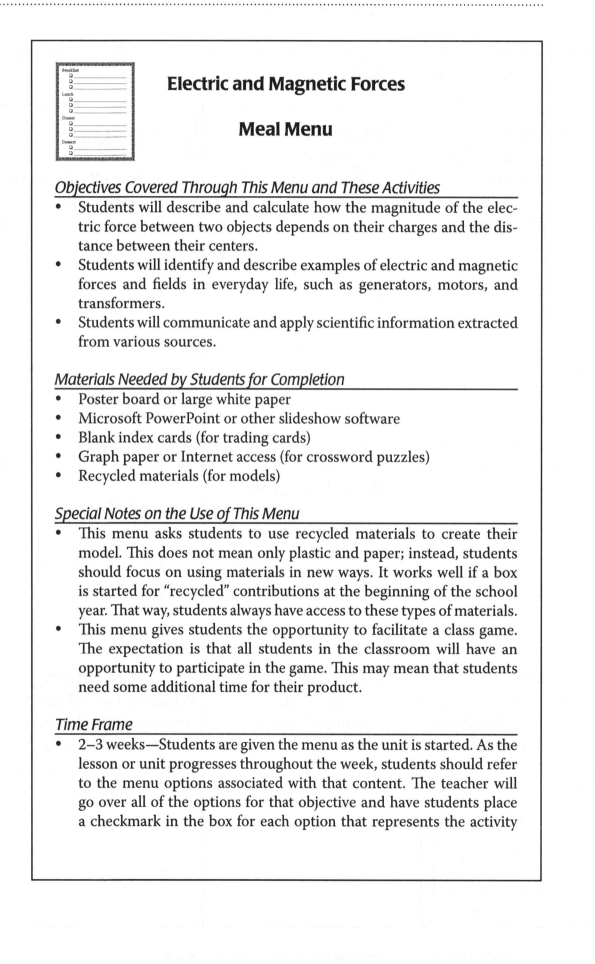

Electric and Magnetic Forces

Meal Menu

Objectives Covered Through This Menu and These Activities

- Students will describe and calculate how the magnitude of the electric force between two objects depends on their charges and the distance between their centers.
- Students will identify and describe examples of electric and magnetic forces and fields in everyday life, such as generators, motors, and transformers.
- Students will communicate and apply scientific information extracted from various sources.

Materials Needed by Students for Completion

- Poster board or large white paper
- Microsoft PowerPoint or other slideshow software
- Blank index cards (for trading cards)
- Graph paper or Internet access (for crossword puzzles)
- Recycled materials (for models)

Special Notes on the Use of This Menu

- This menu asks students to use recycled materials to create their model. This does not mean only plastic and paper; instead, students should focus on using materials in new ways. It works well if a box is started for "recycled" contributions at the beginning of the school year. That way, students always have access to these types of materials.
- This menu gives students the opportunity to facilitate a class game. The expectation is that all students in the classroom will have an opportunity to participate in the game. This may mean that students need some additional time for their product.

Time Frame

- 2–3 weeks—Students are given the menu as the unit is started. As the lesson or unit progresses throughout the week, students should refer to the menu options associated with that content. The teacher will go over all of the options for that objective and have students place a checkmark in the box for each option that represents the activity they are most interested in completing. As teaching continues, the activities chosen and completed should create a full day's meal, with a breakfast, a lunch, and a dinner. The teacher may choose to allow students time to work after other work is finished. When students complete the menu with this expectation, they have completed one activity from each content area, learning style, or level of Bloom's revised taxonomy, depending on the design of the menu.

- 1 week—At the start of the unit, the teacher chooses one activity from each meal family they feel is most valuable for students. Stations can be set up in the classroom. These three activities are available for student choice throughout the week as regular instruction takes place.
- 1–2 days—The teacher chooses an activity or product from an objective to use with the entire class during that lesson time. Additionally, the teacher could choose one of the two desserts as an enrichment activity.

Suggested Forms

- All-purpose rubric
- Free-choice proposal form
- Presentation rubric

Name:_____ Date:_____

Electric and Magnetic Forces

Directions: Choose an activity from each meal below. You must complete these activities in order, progressing from breakfast, to lunch, and then dinner. Place a checkmark next to each box to show which activities you will complete. All activities must be completed by: _____ .

Breakfast

❐ Prepare a stand-alone PowerPoint presentation that shares how magnetic fields are used in generators.

❐ Draw a Venn diagram to compare electric motors with gas engines.

❐ Create a set of trading cards for the different types of transformers. Include how each transformer uses fields and forces.

Lunch

❐ Build a model that demonstrates how to calculate the magnitude of an electric force between objects.

❐ Develop a crossword puzzle in which players answer conceptual questions about how distance, mass, and charges affect electric forces.

❐ Design a folded quiz book with original real-world word problems that require understanding forces and their magnitudes.

Dinner

❐ Select a generator or motor on the market you would like to improve or enhance. Propose an advertisement that shares your improved machine, including appropriate calculations.

❐ Invent a class game that could help your classmates practice real-world situations and calculations related to electric and magnetic forces.

❐ **Free choice on electric and magnetic forces**—Prepare a proposal form and submit it to your teacher for approval.

CHAPTER 7

Energy

Work and Power

Tic-Tac-Toe Menu

Objectives Covered Through This Menu and These Activities
- Students will understand that kinetic energy impacts work.
- Students will be able to distinguish examples of work.
- Students will calculate work and power.
- Students will express, manipulate, and interpret relationships to make predictions and solve problems mathematically.
- Students will communicate valid conclusions supported by data or calculations.
- Students will communicate and apply scientific information extracted from various sources.

Materials Needed by Students for Completion
- Poster board or large white paper
- Recording software or application (for news reports)
- Blank index cards (for card sorts)
- Method for recording responses to word problems

Special Notes on the Use of This Menu
- This menu is a product and problem menu; it asks students to not only create products to demonstrate their knowledge, but also answer one or more higher level word problems. It is set up in such a way that students will have to complete at least one of the word problems. When introducing this menu, teachers will need to have already determined how they would like these problems completed and recorded for grading. Remember, this is the opportunity to hold high standards when it comes to showing work and defending answers!
- This menu gives students the opportunity to create a news report. The grading and sharing of these products can often be facilitated by having students prerecord their product using whatever technology is most convenient for the teacher. This allows the teacher to decide when it will be shown as well as keeps the presentation to its intended length. If recording options are limited, this activity can be modified by allowing students to act out the product (like a play) in front of the class.

Time Frame

- 2–3 weeks—Students are given the menu as the unit is started. The teacher will go over all of the options for that content and have students place checkmarks in the boxes that represent the activities they are most interested in completing. As students choose activities, they should complete a column or a row. When students complete this pattern, they have completed one activity from each content area, learning style, or level of Bloom's revised taxonomy, depending on the design of the menu. As the teacher presents lessons throughout the week, they should refer back to the menu options associated with that content.
- 1 week—At the start of the unit, the teacher chooses the three activities they feel are most valuable for students. Stations can be set up in the classroom. These three activities are available for student choice throughout the week as regular instruction takes place.
- 1–2 days—The teacher chooses an activity from the menu to use with the entire class.

Suggested Forms

- All-purpose rubric
- Free-choice proposal form
- Presentation rubric

Answers to Menu Problems

Problem 1: A person with a mass of 71 kg gets on an elevator. The person rides the elevator up for six floors. If each floor is approximately 3 m high and the trip took about 11 s, how much power was used?

$$P = \frac{W}{T}$$
$$W = Fd$$
$$F = ma \text{ or } F = m\Delta x$$
$$F = 696\,N$$
$$W = 696\,N \cdot 18\,m$$
$$W = 12,528\,J$$
$$P = \frac{12,528\,J}{11\,s}$$
$$P = 1,139\,W$$

1,139 W or 1.139 kW of power were used.

Problem 2: If a line painter for a football stadium uses 110 N of force at an angle of 32° with respect to the horizontal to push the painting machine the length of the field (120 yd) twice for 45 min before the game, how much power is used?

$$P = \frac{W}{T}$$

$$W = Fd$$

$$W = F \cdot \cos\theta \cdot d$$

$$1 \text{ yard} = 0.91 \text{ m}$$

$$W = 110 \text{ N} \cdot \cos 32°(240 \text{ yd} \cdot .91 \text{ m})$$

$$W = (110 \text{ N})(.8480)(218.4 \text{ m})$$

$$W = 20,372 \text{ J}$$

$$45 \text{ min} = 2,700 \text{ s}$$

$$P = \frac{20,372}{2,700 \text{ s}} \doteq 7.6 \text{ W}$$

The painter used approximately 7.6 watts of power.

Problem 3: Two teenagers pushed a stopped car out of traffic. They had to push the 1,190 kg car 300 ft into a parking lot. If each teenager pushed with same force and it took 3 min to move the car, how must power did each provide?

$$P = \frac{W}{T}$$

$$W = Fd$$

$$F = ma$$

$$1 \text{ ft} = .3 \text{ m}$$

$$F_w = 1,190 \text{ kg} \cdot 9.8 \text{ m} / \text{s}^2$$

$$F_w = 11,662 \text{ N}$$

$$W = 11,662 \text{ N} \cdot 90 \text{ m}$$

$$W = 1,049,580 \text{ J}$$

$$P = \frac{1,049,580 \text{ J}}{180 \text{ s}} = \frac{5,831 \text{ W}}{2} = 2,915.5 \text{ W}$$

They used 2,915.5 W (or 2.916 kW) each.

Work and Power

Directions: Check the boxes you plan to complete. They should form a tic-tac-toe across or down. All products are due by: _____ .

☐ *Kinetic Energy and Work* Record a news report in which you report about a sporting event, sharing how different levels of kinetic energy are impacting the amount of work done by participants.	☐ *Problem 1* A person with a mass of 71 kg gets on an elevator. The person rides the elevator up for six floors. If each floor is approximately 3 m high and the trip took about 11 s, how much power was used?	☐ *What Is Work?* Keep a diary for a 12-hour period in which you record each time you are working (physically speaking). Provide a short defense for each action that you note in the diary.
☐ *What Is Work?* Create a card sort that your classmates could use to sort examples and nonexamples of work. Include some tricky situations!	☐ **Free Choice: Kinetic Energy and Work** (Fill out your proposal form before beginning the free choice!)	☐ *Problem 2* If a line painter for a football stadium uses 110 N of force at an angle of 32° with respect to the horizontal to push the painting machine the length of the field (120 yd) twice for 45 min before the game, how much power is used?
☐ *Problem 3* Two teenagers pushed a stopped car out of traffic. They had to push the 1,190 kg car 300 ft into a parking lot. If each teenager pushed with same force and it took 3 min to move the car, how must power did each provide?	☐ *What Is Work?* Select a children's story and underline all of the work that is done in the story. Include a short explanation for each action you underline.	☐ *Kinetic Energy and Work* Prepare a poster that shows how the amount of kinetic energy impacts the amount of work done. Include at least two real-world calculations to support your examples.

<table>
<tr><td>

20 Points
- ☐ _____
- ☐ _____

50 Points
- ☐ _____
- ☐ _____
- ☐ _____
- ☐ _____

80 Points
- ☐ _____
- ☐ _____

</td>
<td>

Energy Transformations

20-50-80 Menu

</td></tr>
</table>

Objectives Covered Through This Menu and These Activities

- Students will describe kinetic and potential energy and their transformations.
- Students will use the law of conservation of energy to describe kinetic and potential energy transformations.
- Students will communicate and apply scientific information extracted from various sources.

Materials Needed by Students for Completion

- Poster board or large white paper
- Blank index cards (for trading cards)
- Large blank lined index cards (for instruction cards)
- Scrapbooking materials (or electronic portfolios)
- Recording software or application (for videos)

Special Notes on the Use of This Menu

- This menu gives students the opportunity to create a video. The grading and sharing of these products can often be facilitated by having students prerecord their product using whatever technology is most convenient for the teacher. This allows the teacher to decide when it will be shown as well as keeps the presentation to its intended length. If recording options are limited, this activity can be modified by allowing students to act out the product (like a play) in front of the class.
- This menu gives students the opportunity to facilitate a class model. The expectation is that all students in the classroom will play an active role in the model. This may mean that students need some additional space for their model.

Time Frame

- 1–2 weeks—Students are given a menu as the unit is started, and the teacher discusses all of the product options on the menu. As the different options are discussed, students will choose the activities they are most interested in completing so that they meet their goal of 100 points. As the lessons progress through the week(s), the teacher and

students refer back to the menu options associated with the content being taught.
- 1–2 days—The teacher chooses an activity or product from the menu to use with the entire class.

Suggested Forms
- All-purpose rubric
- Proposal form for point-based projects
- Presentation rubric

Name:_____ Date:_____

Energy Transformations

Directions: Choose at least two activities from the menu below. The activities must total 100 points. Place a checkmark next to each box to show which activities you will complete. All activities must be completed by _____ .

---

20 Points

❑ Prepare a set of trading cards for all of the formulas associated with kinetic and potential energy and their transformations. Be sure to include the units for each variable and an example on each card.

❑ Write an instruction card that explains how to determine whether an object has kinetic energy, potential energy, or both.

---

50 Points

❑ Research a machine that converts potential energy to kinetic energy. Design a product that shows how the machine depends on this conversion and what forces might make the energy conversion less efficient.

❑ Build a classroom model that demonstrates potential and kinetic energy conversion. Create an original energy conversion problem using realistic units to accompany your model.

❑ Assemble a scrapbook of potential and kinetic energy examples in our everyday lives. Each page should describe the energy source, how that energy might change, and possible values for different forces and energies in the picture.

❑ **Free choice on potential and kinetic energy transformations**—Prepare a proposal form and submit it to your teacher for approval.

---

80 Points

❑ Record an informational video in which you teach others about potential and kinetic energy transformations as well as the law of conservation of energy in the world around us.

❑ Design a graphic novel about a superhero who converts potential and kinetic energy as part of their superpower. Your novel should share how each energy is created and numerical values to explain the physics behind the hero's abilities.

© Prufrock Press Inc. • *Differentiating Instruction With Menus: Physics* • Grades 9–12

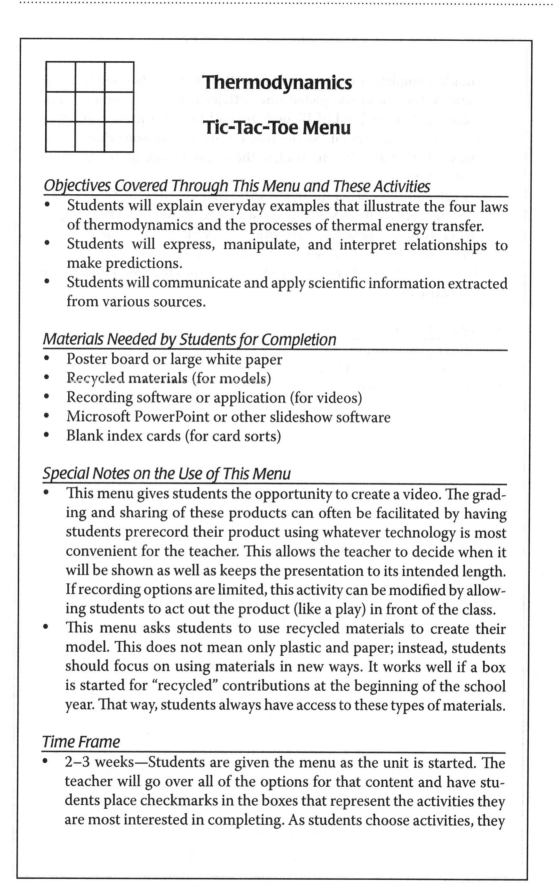

Thermodynamics

Tic-Tac-Toe Menu

Objectives Covered Through This Menu and These Activities

- Students will explain everyday examples that illustrate the four laws of thermodynamics and the processes of thermal energy transfer.
- Students will express, manipulate, and interpret relationships to make predictions.
- Students will communicate and apply scientific information extracted from various sources.

Materials Needed by Students for Completion

- Poster board or large white paper
- Recycled materials (for models)
- Recording software or application (for videos)
- Microsoft PowerPoint or other slideshow software
- Blank index cards (for card sorts)

Special Notes on the Use of This Menu

- This menu gives students the opportunity to create a video. The grading and sharing of these products can often be facilitated by having students prerecord their product using whatever technology is most convenient for the teacher. This allows the teacher to decide when it will be shown as well as keeps the presentation to its intended length. If recording options are limited, this activity can be modified by allowing students to act out the product (like a play) in front of the class.
- This menu asks students to use recycled materials to create their model. This does not mean only plastic and paper; instead, students should focus on using materials in new ways. It works well if a box is started for "recycled" contributions at the beginning of the school year. That way, students always have access to these types of materials.

Time Frame

- 2–3 weeks—Students are given the menu as the unit is started. The teacher will go over all of the options for that content and have students place checkmarks in the boxes that represent the activities they are most interested in completing. As students choose activities, they should complete a column or a row. When students complete this pattern, they have completed one activity from each content area, learning style, or level of Bloom's revised taxonomy, depending on the design of the menu. As the teacher presents lessons throughout the week, they should refer back to the menu options associated with that content.

- 1 week—At the start of the unit, the teacher chooses the three activities they feel are most valuable for students. Stations can be set up in the classroom. These three activities are available for student choice throughout the week as regular instruction takes place.
- 1–2 days—The teacher chooses an activity from the menu to use with the entire class.

Suggested Forms

- All-purpose rubric
- Free-choice proposal form
- Presentation rubric

Thermodynamics

Directions: Check the boxes you plan to complete. They should form a tic-tac-toe across or down. All products are due by: _____ .

☐ *Laws of Thermodynamics* Write and perform an original song to help others understand the different laws of thermodynamics.	☐ *Thermal Energy Transfer* Draw a windowpane that shares descriptions and drawings of thermal energy transfers.	☐ *Zeroth Law* This law has been compared to the algebraic transitive property of equality. Make a model to show why students may say this comparison is true.
☐ *Second Law* Research real-world examples of the second law of thermodynamics. Write an essay that shares your findings.	☐ **Free Choice: Laws of Thermodynamics** (Fill out your proposal form before beginning the free choice!)	☐ *Thermal Energy Transfer* Record an instructional video that shows examples of at least six different types of thermal energy transfers and how each is related to thermodynamics.
☐ *Thermal Energy Transfer* Create a poster that shows examples of entropy and its relationship to energy transfers.	☐ *First Law* Some students say that this law is the same as the law of conservation of energy. Do you agree? Prepare a PowerPoint presentation that proves your opinion.	☐ *Laws of Thermodynamics* Assemble a card sort in which players match real-world examples of each thermodynamic law with the law's number.

Mass-Energy Equivalence

Meal Menu

Objectives Covered Through This Menu and These Activities

- Students will calculate and describe the applications of mass-energy equivalence.
- Students will express, manipulate, and interpret relationships to make predictions and solve problems mathematically.
- Students will communicate valid conclusions supported by data or calculations.
- Students will explain the impacts of contributions of scientists on scientific thought and society.
- Students will describe the history of physics and contributions of physicists.

Materials Needed by Students for Completion

- Poster board or large white paper
- Recording software or application (for videos)
- Microsoft PowerPoint or other slideshow software
- Method for recording responses to word problems

Special Notes on the Use of This Menu

- This menu is a product and problem menu; it asks students to not only create products to demonstrate their knowledge, but also answer one or more higher level word problems. It is set up in such a way that students will have to complete at least one of the word problems. When introducing this menu, teachers will need to have already determined how they would like these problems completed and recorded for grading. Remember, this is the opportunity to hold high standards when it comes to showing work and defending answers!
- This menu gives students the opportunity to create a video. The grading and sharing of these products can often be facilitated by having students prerecord their product using whatever technology is most convenient for the teacher. This allows the teacher to decide when it will be shown as well as keeps the presentation to its intended length. If recording options are limited, this activity can be modified by allowing students to act out the product (like a play) in front of the class.

- This menu gives students the opportunity to present a concept. This can take a significant amount of time and organization. It can save time if the students who choose to do a lesson can sign up for a designated day and time that is determined when the menu is distributed.

Time Frame

- 2–3 weeks—Students are given the menu as the unit is started. As the lesson or unit progresses throughout the week, students should refer to the menu options associated with that content. The teacher will go over all of the options for that objective and have students place a checkmark in the box for each option that represents the activity they are most interested in completing. As teaching continues, the activities chosen and completed should create a full day's meal, with a breakfast, a lunch, and a dinner. The teacher may choose to allow students time to work after other work is finished. When students complete the menu with this expectation, they have completed one activity from each content area, learning style, or level of Bloom's revised taxonomy, depending on the design of the menu.
- 1 week—At the start of the unit, the teacher chooses one activity from each meal family they feel are most valuable for students. Stations can be set up in the classroom. These three activities are available for student choice throughout the week as regular instruction takes place.
- 1–2 days—The teacher chooses an activity or product from an objective to use with the entire class during that lesson time. Additionally, the teacher could choose one of the two desserts as an enrichment activity.

Suggested Forms

- All-purpose rubric
- Free-choice proposal form
- Presentation rubric

Answers to Menu Problems

Problem 1: If 100 g of nitrogen were used to power a 2,540 kg rocket, how fast would the rocket move, assuming all of the nitrogen was converted into the rocket's kinetic energy?

$$E = mc^2$$

$$E = (.1\,\text{kg})(3 \times 10^8\,\text{m/s})^2$$

$$E = 9 \times 10^{15}\,\text{J}$$

$$E_k = \frac{mv^2}{2}$$

$$2 \left[9 \times 10^{15}\,\text{J} = \frac{(2,540\,\text{kg})(v^2)}{2} \right]$$

$$\frac{1.8 \times 10^6\,\text{J}}{2,540\,\text{kg}} = \frac{(2,540\,\text{kg})(v^2)}{2,540\,\text{kg}}$$

$$7.1 \times 10^{12} = v^2$$

$$2.7 \times 10^6\,\text{m/s}$$

The answer is 2.7×10^6 m/s.

Problem 2: If a bomb converted 3.2×10^{-4} g of its mass to energy, how much energy was released? Is this more or less energy than the Little Boy atomic bomb produced?

$$E = mc^2$$

$$E = 3.2 \times 10^{-4}\,\text{g or } 3.2 \times 10^{-7}\,\text{kg}$$

$$E = (3.2 \times 10^{-7}\,\text{kg})(3 \times 10^8\,\text{m/s})^2$$

$$E = 2.88 \times 10^{10}\,\text{J}$$

Little Boy had approximately 6.3×10^{13} J of energy, so this bomb did not produce as much energy.

Problem 3: The Fat Man atomic bomb exploded with about 84 TJ of energy. How many grams of mass must have been converted in the explosion?

$$84 \text{ TJ} = 8.3 \times 10^{13} \text{ J}$$

$$E = mc^2$$

$$8.3 \times 10^{13} \text{ J} = m(3 \times 10^8 \text{ m / s})^2$$

$$\frac{8.3 \times 10^{13} \text{ J}}{9 \times 10^{16} \text{ m / s}} = \frac{m(9 \times 10^{16} \text{ m / s})}{9 \times 10^{16} \text{ m / s}}$$

$$9.2 \times 10^{-4} \text{ kg} = m$$

Approximately .9 g of mass were converted to energy.

Name:_____ Date:_____

Mass-Energy Equivalence

Directions: Choose an activity from each meal below. You must complete these activities in order, progressing from breakfast, to lunch, and then dinner. Place a checkmark next to each box to show which activities you will complete. All activities must be completed by: _____ .

Breakfast

❏ Research the mass-energy equivalence. Create a decorative poster to share your findings.

❏ Design an appropriate greeting card thanking the researcher credited with the mass-energy equivalence for their work.

❏ **Free choice on using mass-energy equivalence**—Prepare a proposal form and submit it to your teacher for approval.

Lunch

❏ **Problem 1:** If 100 g of nitrogen were used to power a 2,540 kg rocket, how fast would the rocket move, assuming all of the nitrogen was converted into the rocket's kinetic energy?

❏ **Problem 2:** If a bomb converted 3.2×10^{-4} g of its mass to energy, how much energy was released? Is this more or less energy than the Little Boy atomic bomb produced?

❏ **Problem 3:** The Fat Man atomic bomb exploded with about 84 TJ of energy. How many grams of mass must have been converted in the explosion?

Dinner

❏ Record an instructional video that teaches others about mass-energy equivalence as it relates to space travel.

❏ Organize a presentation in which participants experience different examples of the mass-energy equivalence in historical events.

❏ Prepare a You Be the Person in which you are the discoverer of the mass-energy equivalence relationship speaking about how your findings have impacted modern physics.

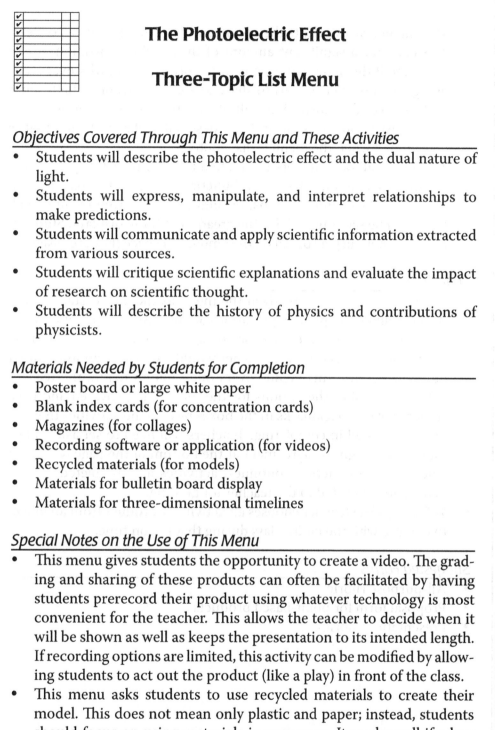

The Photoelectric Effect

Three-Topic List Menu

Objectives Covered Through This Menu and These Activities
- Students will describe the photoelectric effect and the dual nature of light.
- Students will express, manipulate, and interpret relationships to make predictions.
- Students will communicate and apply scientific information extracted from various sources.
- Students will critique scientific explanations and evaluate the impact of research on scientific thought.
- Students will describe the history of physics and contributions of physicists.

Materials Needed by Students for Completion
- Poster board or large white paper
- Blank index cards (for concentration cards)
- Magazines (for collages)
- Recording software or application (for videos)
- Recycled materials (for models)
- Materials for bulletin board display
- Materials for three-dimensional timelines

Special Notes on the Use of This Menu
- This menu gives students the opportunity to create a video. The grading and sharing of these products can often be facilitated by having students prerecord their product using whatever technology is most convenient for the teacher. This allows the teacher to decide when it will be shown as well as keeps the presentation to its intended length. If recording options are limited, this activity can be modified by allowing students to act out the product (like a play) in front of the class.
- This menu asks students to use recycled materials to create their model. This does not mean only plastic and paper; instead, students should focus on using materials in new ways. It works well if a box is started for "recycled" contributions at the beginning of the school year. That way, students always have access to these types of materials.

- This menu gives students the opportunity to demonstrate a concept. This can take a significant amount of time and organization. It can save time if the demonstration is prerecorded (using whatever technology is most convenient) to share at a later time, or if the teacher prefers "live" demonstrations, all of the students who choose to do a demonstration can sign up for a designated day and time that is determined when the menu is distributed.
- This menu allows students to create a bulletin board display. Some classrooms may only have one bulletin board, so the teacher can divide the board into sections, or additional classroom wall or hall space can be sectioned off for the creation of these displays. Students can plan their display based on the amount of space they are assigned.

Time Frame

- 1–2 weeks—Students are given the menu as the unit is started, and the guidelines and point expectations are discussed. Students usually will need to earn 100 points for 100%, although there is an opportunity for extra credit if the teacher would like to use another target number. Because this menu covers one topic in depth, the teacher will go over all of the options for the topic being covered and have students place checkmarks in the boxes next to the activities they are most interested in completing. Teachers will need to set aside a few moments to sign the agreement at the bottom of the page with each student. As instruction continues, activities are completed by students and submitted to the teacher for grading.
- 1–2 days—The teacher chooses an activity or product from an objective to use with the entire class during that lesson time.

Suggested Forms

- All-purpose rubric
- Proposal form for point-based products
- Presentation rubric

Name:_____ Date:_____

The Photoelectric Effect

Guidelines:

1. You may complete as many of the activities listed as you wish within the time period.
2. You may choose any combination of activities, but **must** complete at least one activity from each topic area.
3. Your goal is 100 points. (This is a grade of 100/100.) You may earn up to _____ points extra credit.
4. You may be as creative as you like within the guidelines listed below.
5. You must show your plan to your teacher by _____ .
6. Activities may be turned in at any time during the working time period. They will be graded and recorded on this sheet as you continue to work, so keep it safe!

Topic	Plan to Do	Activity to Complete	Point Value	Date Completed	Points Earned
Light as Waves		Design a set of concentration cards in which players match drawings of light behavior with the term for each behavior.	15		
		Create a collage of pictures of everyday events that support the idea that light is a wave.	15		
		Perform a demonstration that shows how light demonstrates various wave behaviors.	20		
		Determine what wave behaviors are not exhibited by light. Record a video that proves your findings.	30		
Light as Particles		Develop Three Facts and a Fib to quiz misconceptions about the behavior of light.	15		
		Build a model that could be used to demonstrate the theory that light travels as particles.	20		
		Design a quiz for your classmates about the theory that light travels as a particle.	25		
		Write a speech that a photon might give when asked to prove whether it is a wave and particle.	30		
Photoelectric Effect		Assemble a bulletin board display or PowerPoint presentation that explains the photoelectric effect.	15		
		Draw a Venn diagram to compare lights behaviors as a wave and a particle.	20		
		Assemble a three-dimensional timeline that shows how theories about light behavior have changed over time.	25		
		Prepare a You Be the Person presentation in which as Maxwell you discuss how your theory is not supported by photoelectric effect observations.	30		
Any		**Free Choice:** Submit your free-choice proposal form for a product of your choice.			
		Total number of points you are planning to earn.	**Total points earned:**		

I am planning to complete _____ activities that could earn up to a total of _____ points.

Teacher's initials _____ Student's signature _____

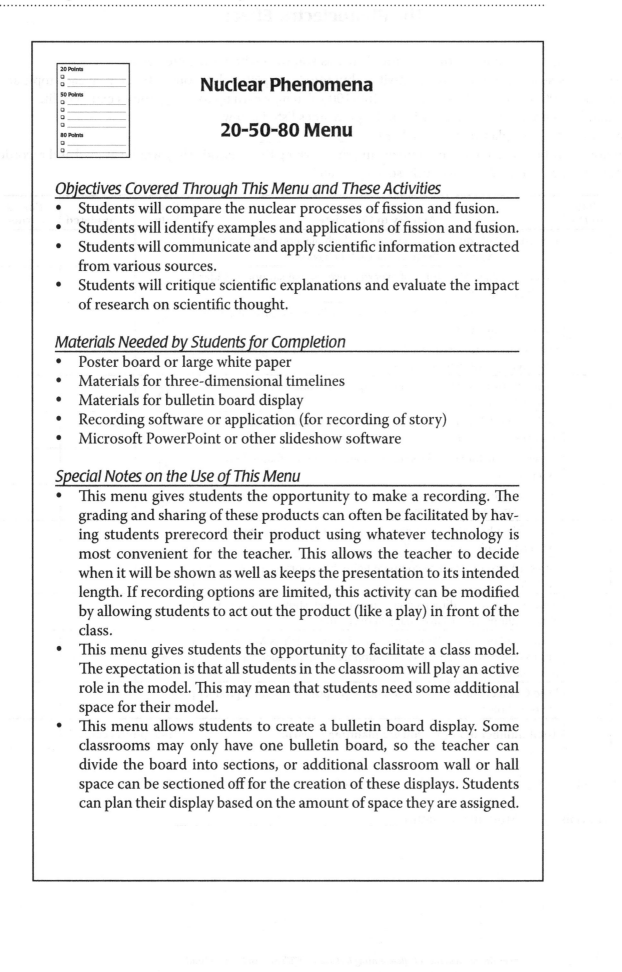

Nuclear Phenomena

20-50-80 Menu

20 Points
- ☐ _____
- ☐ _____

50 Points
- ☐ _____
- ☐ _____
- ☐ _____
- ☐ _____

80 Points
- ☐ _____
- ☐ _____

Objectives Covered Through This Menu and These Activities
- Students will compare the nuclear processes of fission and fusion.
- Students will identify examples and applications of fission and fusion.
- Students will communicate and apply scientific information extracted from various sources.
- Students will critique scientific explanations and evaluate the impact of research on scientific thought.

Materials Needed by Students for Completion
- Poster board or large white paper
- Materials for three-dimensional timelines
- Materials for bulletin board display
- Recording software or application (for recording of story)
- Microsoft PowerPoint or other slideshow software

Special Notes on the Use of This Menu
- This menu gives students the opportunity to make a recording. The grading and sharing of these products can often be facilitated by having students prerecord their product using whatever technology is most convenient for the teacher. This allows the teacher to decide when it will be shown as well as keeps the presentation to its intended length. If recording options are limited, this activity can be modified by allowing students to act out the product (like a play) in front of the class.
- This menu gives students the opportunity to facilitate a class model. The expectation is that all students in the classroom will play an active role in the model. This may mean that students need some additional space for their model.
- This menu allows students to create a bulletin board display. Some classrooms may only have one bulletin board, so the teacher can divide the board into sections, or additional classroom wall or hall space can be sectioned off for the creation of these displays. Students can plan their display based on the amount of space they are assigned.

Time Frame

- 1–2 weeks—Students are given a menu as the unit is started, and the teacher discusses all of the product options on the menu. As the different options are discussed, students will choose the activities they are most interested in completing so that they meet their goal of 100 points. As the lessons progress through the week(s), the teacher and students refer back to the menu options associated with the content being taught.
- 1–2 days—The teacher chooses an activity or product from the menu to use with the entire class.

Suggested Forms

- All-purpose rubric
- Proposal form for point-based projects
- Presentation rubric

Name:_____ Date:_____

Nuclear Phenomena

Directions: Choose at least two activities from the menu below. The activities must total 100 points. Place a checkmark next to each box to show which activities you will complete. All activities must be completed by _____ .

---

20 Points

☐ Draw a thematic Venn diagram to compare the processes of fission and fusion.

☐ Prepare a class model that demonstrates the fission and fusion processes.

---

50 Points

☐ Build a three-dimensional timeline for research in the areas of fission and fusion.

☐ Research nuclear power plants and design a bulletin board display that advertises the benefits of fission plants.

☐ Create a social media profile for a radioactive element that is vital to nuclear reactions.

☐ **Free choice on applications of nuclear fission and fusion**—Prepare a proposal form and submit it to your teacher for approval.

---

80 Points

☐ Write (or record) a science-based story about a community that lives on a planet without fusion reactions.

☐ Interview a physicist about the importance of fission or fusion. Using their responses, determine which reaction has the bigger daily impact on our lives and record a presentation to share your views.

CHAPTER 8

Waves

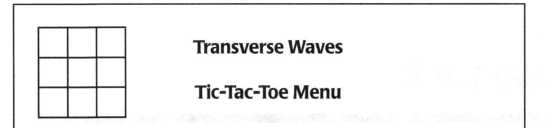

Transverse Waves

Tic-Tac-Toe Menu

Objectives Covered Through This Menu and These Activities
- Students will compare characteristics and behaviors of transverse waves, including electromagnetic waves and the electromagnetic spectrum.
- Students will express, manipulate, and interpret relationships to make predictions.
- Students will communicate and apply scientific information extracted from various sources.

Materials Needed by Students for Completion
- Poster board or large white paper
- Blank index cards (for trading cards)
- Recording software or application (for videos)
- Graph paper or Internet access (for WebQuests)

Special Notes on the Use of This Menu
- This menu gives students the opportunity to create a video. The grading and sharing of these products can often be facilitated by having students prerecord their product using whatever technology is most convenient for the teacher. This allows the teacher to decide when it will be shown as well as keeps the presentation to its intended length. If recording options are limited, this activity can be modified by allowing students to act out the product (like a play) in front of the class.
- This menu gives students the opportunity to facilitate a class model. The expectation is that all students in the classroom will play an active role in the model. This may mean that students need some additional space for their model.
- This menu allows students to create a WebQuest. There are multiple versions and templates for WebQuests available on the Internet. It is your decision whether you would like to specify a format or if you will allow students to create one of their own choosing.

Time Frame

- 2–3 weeks—Students are given the menu as the unit is started. The teacher will go over all of the options for that content and have students place checkmarks in the boxes that represent the activities they are most interested in completing. As students choose activities, they should complete a column or a row. When students complete this pattern, they have completed one activity from each content area, learning style, or level of Bloom's revised taxonomy, depending on the design of the menu. As the teacher presents lessons throughout the week, they should refer back to the menu options associated with that content.
- 1 week—At the start of the unit, the teacher chooses the three activities they feel are most valuable for students. Stations can be set up in the classroom. These three activities are available for student choice throughout the week as regular instruction takes place.
- 1–2 days—The teacher chooses an activity from the menu to use with the entire class.

Suggested Forms

- All-purpose rubric
- Free-choice proposal form
- Presentation rubric

Name:_____ Date:_____

Transverse Waves

Directions: Check the boxes you plan to complete. They should form a tic-tac-toe across or down. All products are due by: _____ .

☐ _Transverse Waves_ Prepare a poster with a transverse wave and its characteristics labeled.	☐ _Behavior of Transverse Waves_ Develop a social media profile for a student who unknowingly posts photos and check-ins that demonstrate the different behaviors of transverse waves.	☐ _Electromagnetic Waves_ Invent a classroom model that could be used to demonstrate the characteristics and behaviors of each wave of the electromagnetic spectrum.
☐ _Electromagnetic Waves_ Create a set of trading cards for the electromagnetic waves found on the electromagnetic spectrum.	☐ **Free Choice: Transverse Waves** (Fill out your proposal form before beginning the free choice!)	☐ _Behavior of Transverse Waves_ Record a video in which you share how the behavior of transverse waves can help detectives be better at their job.
☐ _Behavior of Transverse Waves_ Write a choose-your-own-adventure story in which different wave behaviors help the reader make decisions.	☐ _Electromagnetic Waves_ Prepare a WebQuest that allows questors to compare the characteristics of the different waves on the electromagnetic spectrum.	☐ _Transverse Waves_ Compose a song with hand motions to teach others about transverse waves and their characteristics.

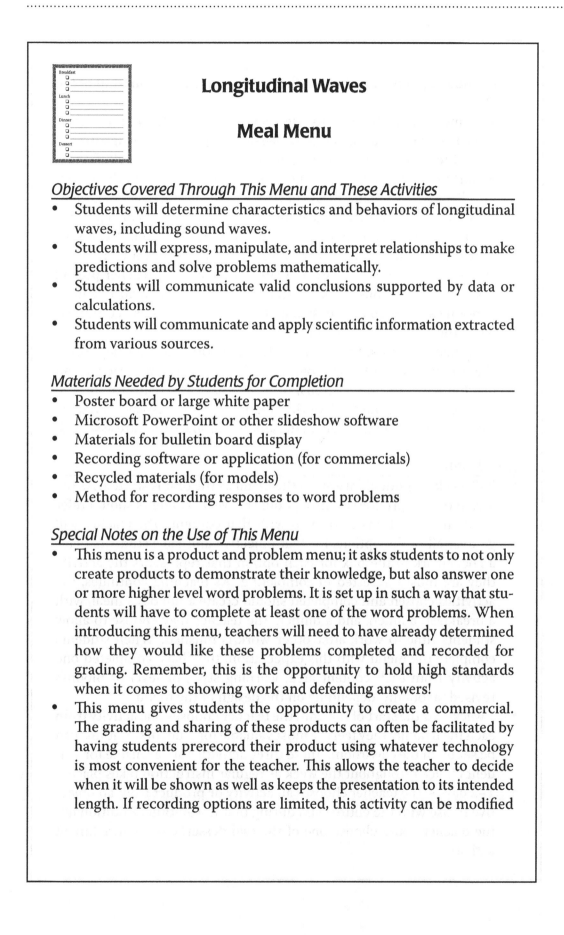

Longitudinal Waves

Meal Menu

Objectives Covered Through This Menu and These Activities

- Students will determine characteristics and behaviors of longitudinal waves, including sound waves.
- Students will express, manipulate, and interpret relationships to make predictions and solve problems mathematically.
- Students will communicate valid conclusions supported by data or calculations.
- Students will communicate and apply scientific information extracted from various sources.

Materials Needed by Students for Completion

- Poster board or large white paper
- Microsoft PowerPoint or other slideshow software
- Materials for bulletin board display
- Recording software or application (for commercials)
- Recycled materials (for models)
- Method for recording responses to word problems

Special Notes on the Use of This Menu

- This menu is a product and problem menu; it asks students to not only create products to demonstrate their knowledge, but also answer one or more higher level word problems. It is set up in such a way that students will have to complete at least one of the word problems. When introducing this menu, teachers will need to have already determined how they would like these problems completed and recorded for grading. Remember, this is the opportunity to hold high standards when it comes to showing work and defending answers!
- This menu gives students the opportunity to create a commercial. The grading and sharing of these products can often be facilitated by having students prerecord their product using whatever technology is most convenient for the teacher. This allows the teacher to decide when it will be shown as well as keeps the presentation to its intended length. If recording options are limited, this activity can be modified

by allowing students to act out the product (like a play) in front of the class.

- This menu asks students to use recycled materials to create their model. This does not mean only plastic and paper; instead, students should focus on using materials in new ways. It works well if a box is started for "recycled" contributions at the beginning of the school year. That way, students always have access to these types of materials.

- This menu gives students the opportunity to present a concept. This can take a significant amount of time and organization. It can save time if the demonstration is prerecorded (using whatever technology is most convenient) to share at a later time, or if the teacher prefers "live" demonstrations, all of the students who choose to do a demonstration can sign up for a designated day and time that is determined when the menu is distributed.

- This menu allows students to create a bulletin board display. Some classrooms may only have one bulletin board, so the teacher can divide the board into sections, or additional classroom wall or hall space can be sectioned off for the creation of these displays. Students can plan their display based on the amount of space they are assigned.

Time Frame

- 2–3 weeks—Students are given the menu as the unit is started. As the lesson or unit progresses throughout the week, students should refer to the menu options associated with that content. The teacher will go over all of the options for that objective and have students place a checkmark in the box for each option that represents the activity they are most interested in completing. As teaching continues, the activities chosen and completed should create a full day's meal, with a breakfast, a lunch, and a dinner. The teacher may choose to allow students time to work after other work is finished. When students complete the menu with this expectation, they have completed one activity from each content area, learning style, or level of Bloom's revised taxonomy, depending on the design of the menu.

- 1 week—At the start of the unit, the teacher chooses one activity from each meal family they feel are most valuable for students. Stations can be set up in the classroom. These three activities are available for student choice throughout the week as regular instruction takes place.

- 1–2 days—The teacher chooses an activity or product from an objective to use with the entire class during that lesson time. Additionally, the teacher could choose one of the two desserts as an enrichment activity.

Suggested Forms
- All-purpose rubric
- Free-choice proposal form
- Presentation rubric

Answers to Menu Problems

Problem 1: If it were possible, how many seconds would it take to hear an echo if you yell toward the other side of the Grand Canyon when the air temperature is 25 °C?

The Grand Canyon is approximately 29 km wide, or a total 58 km or 58,000 m.

The speed of sound through air at 25 °C is 346 m/s.

$$v = \frac{d}{t}$$

$$346 \, \text{m/s} = \frac{58,000 \, \text{m}}{t}$$

$$t = \frac{58,000 \, \text{m}}{346 \, \text{m/s}} = 168 \, \text{s or 2.8 min}$$

If possible, the echo would return in 168 s or 2.8 min.

Problem 2: If a person sees someone in their neighborhood hammering a nail into their fence on a 20 °C day, the sound of the hammer comes .03 s after they see their neighbor hit the nail. How far away is the neighbor?

The speed of sound at 20 °C is about 343 m/s.

$$v = \frac{d}{t}$$

$$vt = d$$

$$(343 \, \text{m/s})(.03 \, \text{s}) = d$$

$$10 \, \text{m} = d$$

The neighbor is 10 m away.

Problem 3: A dolphin uses its echolocation to pinpoint a shark about 123 m away. How long will it take for a sound wave to travel to the shark and back to the dolphin?

$$v = \frac{d}{t}$$

$$1{,}500 \text{ m / s} = \frac{246 \text{ m}}{t}$$

$$t = \frac{246 \text{ m}}{1{,}500 \text{ m / s}} = .164 \text{ s}$$

It would take about .164 s.

Name:_____ Date:_____

Longitudinal Waves

Directions: Choose an activity from each meal below. You must complete these activities in order, progressing from breakfast, to lunch, and then dinner. Place a checkmark next to each box to show which activities you will complete. All activities must be completed by: _____ .

Breakfast

❑ Prepare a PowerPoint presentation that features video examples of different real-world longitudinal wave behaviors.

❑ Consider different examples of longitudinal waves we experience daily. Assemble a bulletin board display about these waves and their behaviors. Label the parts of each wave on your display.

❑ **Free choice on longitudinal wave features and behaviors**—Prepare a proposal form and submit it to your teacher for approval.

Lunch

❑ **Problem 1:** If it were possible, how many seconds would it take to hear an echo if you yell toward the other side of the Grand Canyon when the air temperature is 25 °C?

❑ **Problem 2:** If a person sees someone in their neighborhood hammering a nail into their fence on a 20 °C day, the sound of the hammer comes .03 s after they see their neighbor hit the nail. How far away is the neighbor?

❑ **Problem 3:** A dolphin uses its echolocation to pinpoint a shark about 123 m away. How long will it take for a sound wave to travel to the shark and back to the dolphin?

Dinner

❑ Make a working model that shows why sound travels at different speeds through different materials.

❑ Record a commercial for a new soundproofing material. It should include the composition of the new material and how it helps stop sound.

❑ Research how scientists use longitudinal wave behavior to track and predict earthquakes. Prepare a presentation that shares the connection you discovered.

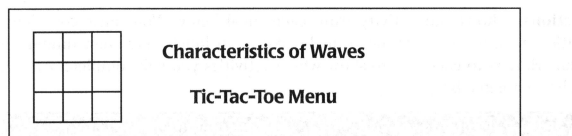

Characteristics of Waves

Tic-Tac-Toe Menu

Objectives Covered Through This Menu and These Activities

- Students will investigate and analyze characteristics of waves, including velocity, frequency, amplitude, and wavelength.
- Students will calculate using the relationship between wave speed, frequency, and wavelength.
- Students will express, manipulate, and interpret relationships to make predictions and solve problems mathematically.
- Students will communicate valid conclusions supported by data or calculations.
- Students will communicate and apply scientific information extracted from various sources.

Materials Needed by Students for Completion

- Poster board or large white paper
- Blank index cards (for concentration cards)
- Recycled materials (for models)
- Method for recording responses to word problems

Special Notes on the Use of This Menu

- This menu is a product and problem menu; it asks students to not only create products to demonstrate their knowledge, but also answer one or more higher level word problems. It is set up in such a way that students will have to complete at least one of the word problems. When introducing this menu, teachers will need to have already determined how they would like these problems completed and recorded for grading. Remember, this is the opportunity to hold high standards when it comes to showing work and defending answers!
- This menu asks students to use recycled materials to create their model. This does not mean only plastic and paper; instead, students should focus on using materials in new ways. It works well if a box is started for "recycled" contributions at the beginning of the school year. That way, students always have access to these types of materials.

Time Frame

- 2–3 weeks—Students are given the menu as the unit is started. The teacher will go over all of the options for that content and have students place checkmarks in the boxes that represent the activities they are most interested in completing. As students choose activities, they should complete a column or a row. When students complete this pattern, they have completed one activity from each content area, learning style, or level of Bloom's revised taxonomy, depending on the design of the menu. As the teacher presents lessons throughout the week, they should refer back to the menu options associated with that content.
- 1 week—At the start of the unit, the teacher chooses the three activities they feel are most valuable for students. Stations can be set up in the classroom. These three activities are available for student choice throughout the week as regular instruction takes place.
- 1–2 days—The teacher chooses an activity from the menu to use with the entire class.

Suggested Forms

- All-purpose rubric
- Free-choice proposal form
- Presentation rubric

Answers to Menu Problems

Problem 1: Waves are hitting the shore at the beach at a rate of 2 waves every second. If the distance between crests is about 1.3 m, how fast are the waves traveling?

$$v = \lambda f$$
$$v = (1.3 \text{ m})(2 \text{ Hz})$$
$$v = 2.6 \text{ m/s}$$

The waves are traveling at 2.6 m/s.

Problem 2: Two students are debating about the color of light being emitted from a screen. The light has an energy of 3.52×10^{-19} J. What is the color of the light?

$$E = hf$$

$$\frac{3.52 \times 10^{-19}}{6.626 \times 10^{-34} \, J} = \frac{(6.626 \times 10^{-34} \, J)(f)}{6.626 \times 10^{-34} \, J}$$

$$5.31 \times 10^{14} \, Hz = f$$

$$c = \lambda f$$

$$\frac{3.0 \times 10^{8} \, m/s}{5.31 \times 10^{14} \, Hz} = \frac{\lambda(5.31 \times 10^{14} \, Hz)}{5.31 \times 10^{14} \, Hz}$$

$$5.65 \times 10^{-7} \, m = \lambda$$

$$565 \, nm = \lambda$$

The light is green.

Problem 3: A boat is anchored in a lake. Waves traveling at a speed of 6.5 m/s rock the boat every 10 s. How far apart are the waves?

$$v = \lambda f$$

$$\frac{6.5 \, m/s}{.1 \, Hz} = \frac{\lambda(.1 \, Hz)}{.1 \, Hz}$$

$$65 \, m = \lambda$$

The wavelength would be 65 m.

Characteristics of Waves

Directions: Check the boxes you plan to complete. They should form a tic-tac-toe across or down. All products are due by: _____ .

☐ *Characteristics of Waves* Write and perform a song with appropriate hand motions that demonstrates the different characteristics of waves.	☐ *Problem 1* Waves are hitting the shore at the beach at a rate of 2 waves every second. If the distance between crests is about 1.3 m, how fast are the waves traveling?	☐ *Conceptual Considerations* Design a folded quiz book that quizzes others about how changing one characteristic of a wave can impact other characteristics.
☐ *Conceptual Considerations* Design a brochure that shows the relationships between speed, wavelength, and frequency in different types of waves.	☐ **Free Choice: Characteristics of Waves** (Fill out your proposal form before beginning the free choice!)	☐ *Problem 2* Two students are debating about the color of light being emitted from a screen. The light has an energy of 3.52×10^{-19} J. What is the color of the light?
☐ *Problem 3* A boat is anchored in a lake. Waves traveling at a speed of 6.5 m/s rock the boat every 10 s. How far apart are the waves?	☐ *Conceptual Considerations* Build a model that could be used to show the relationship between frequency, wavelength, and speed.	☐ *Characteristics of Waves* Create a set of concentration cards for the characteristics of waves and the different measurements that affect them.

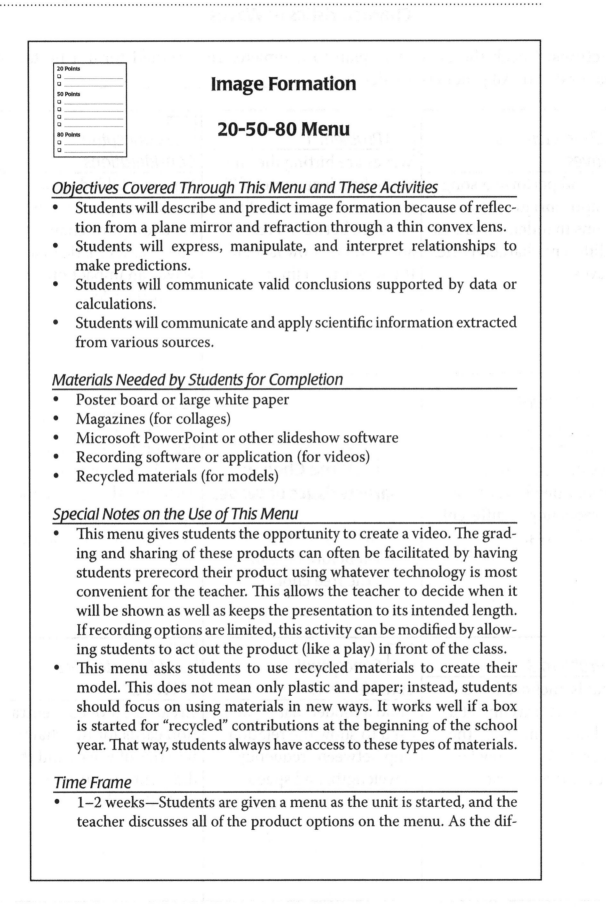

Image Formation

20-50-80 Menu

20 Points
☐ _____
☐ _____
50 Points
☐ _____
☐ _____
☐ _____
80 Points
☐ _____
☐ _____

Objectives Covered Through This Menu and These Activities
- Students will describe and predict image formation because of reflection from a plane mirror and refraction through a thin convex lens.
- Students will express, manipulate, and interpret relationships to make predictions.
- Students will communicate valid conclusions supported by data or calculations.
- Students will communicate and apply scientific information extracted from various sources.

Materials Needed by Students for Completion
- Poster board or large white paper
- Magazines (for collages)
- Microsoft PowerPoint or other slideshow software
- Recording software or application (for videos)
- Recycled materials (for models)

Special Notes on the Use of This Menu
- This menu gives students the opportunity to create a video. The grading and sharing of these products can often be facilitated by having students prerecord their product using whatever technology is most convenient for the teacher. This allows the teacher to decide when it will be shown as well as keeps the presentation to its intended length. If recording options are limited, this activity can be modified by allowing students to act out the product (like a play) in front of the class.
- This menu asks students to use recycled materials to create their model. This does not mean only plastic and paper; instead, students should focus on using materials in new ways. It works well if a box is started for "recycled" contributions at the beginning of the school year. That way, students always have access to these types of materials.

Time Frame
- 1–2 weeks—Students are given a menu as the unit is started, and the teacher discusses all of the product options on the menu. As the dif-

ferent options are discussed, students will choose the activities they are most interested in completing so that they meet their goal of 100 points. As the lessons progress through the week(s), the teacher and students refer back to the menu options associated with the content being taught.

- 1–2 days—The teacher chooses an activity or product from the menu to use with the entire class.

Suggested Forms

- All-purpose rubric
- Proposal form for point-based projects
- Presentation rubric

Image Formation

Directions: Choose at least two activities from the menu below. The activities must total 100 points. Place a checkmark next to each box to show which activities you will complete. All activities must be completed by _____ .

---

20 Points

❑ Create a collage of examples of images created by reflection and refraction in the world around us.

❑ Prepare a poster that explains the physical laws associated with reflection from a plane mirror and refraction through a convex lens.

---

50 Points

❑ Design an advertisement or commercial for a modern-day product that relies on reflection or refraction to form an image. Be sure to include how the product produces the image.

❑ Keep a diary or journal for 3 days of reflections and refractions you see. Each entry should include a drawing that shows how each image was formed.

❑ Record a video that could teach others how to predict images created by reflection and refraction.

❑ **Free choice on images created through reflection and refraction—** Prepare a proposal form and submit it to your teacher for approval.

---

80 Points

❑ Research amusement park attractions that use mirrors and lens. Design a model of an attraction that uses both to create a unique experience. Your model should indicate where visitors will stand and what kinds of images will be created.

❑ Research the use of mirrored surfaces in artwork and architecture. Prepare a PowerPoint presentation or bulletin board display to illustrate how images created by these surfaces add to their aesthetic.

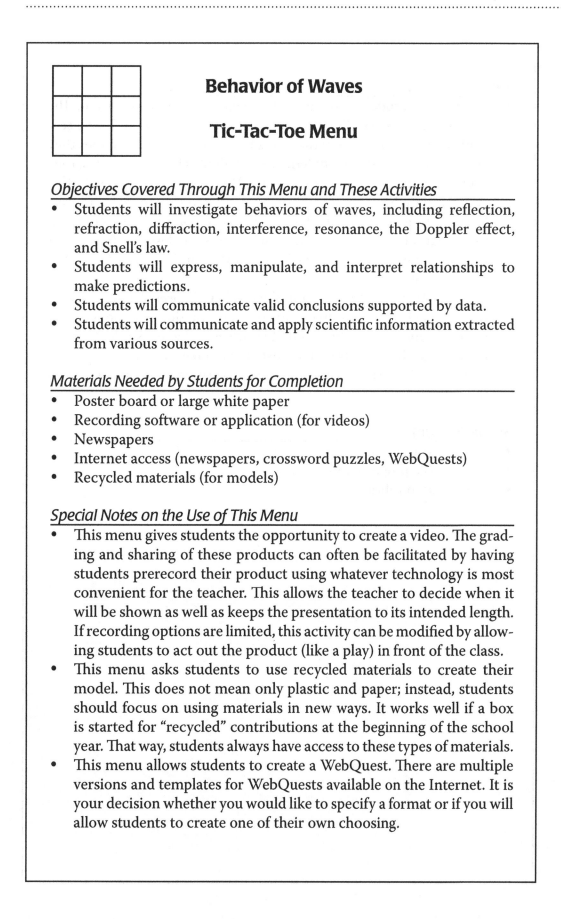

Behavior of Waves

Tic-Tac-Toe Menu

Objectives Covered Through This Menu and These Activities
- Students will investigate behaviors of waves, including reflection, refraction, diffraction, interference, resonance, the Doppler effect, and Snell's law.
- Students will express, manipulate, and interpret relationships to make predictions.
- Students will communicate valid conclusions supported by data.
- Students will communicate and apply scientific information extracted from various sources.

Materials Needed by Students for Completion
- Poster board or large white paper
- Recording software or application (for videos)
- Newspapers
- Internet access (newspapers, crossword puzzles, WebQuests)
- Recycled materials (for models)

Special Notes on the Use of This Menu
- This menu gives students the opportunity to create a video. The grading and sharing of these products can often be facilitated by having students prerecord their product using whatever technology is most convenient for the teacher. This allows the teacher to decide when it will be shown as well as keeps the presentation to its intended length. If recording options are limited, this activity can be modified by allowing students to act out the product (like a play) in front of the class.
- This menu asks students to use recycled materials to create their model. This does not mean only plastic and paper; instead, students should focus on using materials in new ways. It works well if a box is started for "recycled" contributions at the beginning of the school year. That way, students always have access to these types of materials.
- This menu allows students to create a WebQuest. There are multiple versions and templates for WebQuests available on the Internet. It is your decision whether you would like to specify a format or if you will allow students to create one of their own choosing.

Time Frame

- 2–3 weeks—Students are given the menu as the unit is started. The teacher will go over all of the options for that content and have students place checkmarks in the boxes that represent the activities they are most interested in completing. As students choose activities, they should complete a column or a row. When students complete this pattern, they have completed one activity from each content area, learning style, or level of Bloom's revised taxonomy, depending on the design of the menu. As the teacher presents lessons throughout the week, they should refer back to the menu options associated with that content.
- 1 week—At the start of the unit, the teacher chooses the three activities they feel are most valuable for students. Stations can be set up in the classroom. These three activities are available for student choice throughout the week as regular instruction takes place.
- 1–2 days—The teacher chooses an activity from the menu to use with the entire class.

Suggested Forms

- All-purpose rubric
- Free-choice proposal form
- Presentation rubric

Name:_____ Date:_____

Behavior of Waves

Directions: Check the boxes you plan to complete. They should form a tic-tac-toe across or down. All products are due by: _____ .

The menus choices are not specific to any one behavior of waves. When you decide on your choices, plan on including all of the following behaviors in your products. For example, if you complete a product that compares two behaviors, then you have completed two behaviors.

- Reflection
- Refraction
- Diffraction
- Snell's Law
- Constructive Interference
- Destructive Interference
- Resonance
- Doppler Effect

☐ *Noting Wave Behaviors*	☐ *Showing Wave Behaviors*	☐ *Seeing Wave Behaviors*
Design a Venn diagram to compare two wave behaviors.	Record an instructional video in which you show or demonstrate different wave behaviors.	Write a children's book in which the main character solves a mystery by understanding the behavior of waves.
☐ *Seeing Wave Behaviors* On a poster, present at least two newspaper articles about recent events that demonstrate wave behaviors. Be sure to explain how each shows the behavior.	☐ **Free Choice: Noting Wave Behaviors** (Fill out your proposal form before beginning the free choice!)	☐ *Showing Wave Behaviors* Build a model that others could use to demonstrate different wave behaviors.
☐ *Showing Wave Behaviors* Prepare a WebQuest that encourages questors to experience wave behaviors that could be easily shown in a classroom or lab environment.	☐ *Seeing Wave Behaviors* Create a crossword puzzle using pictures of wave properties and real-world wave behaviors as clues.	☐ *Noting Wave Behaviors* Make a foldable that shares unique information about the different wave behaviors as well as any associated calculations.

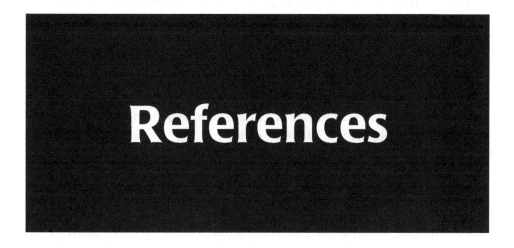

References

Anderson, L., & Krathwohl, D. R. (Eds.). (2001). *A taxonomy for learning, teaching, and assessing: A revision of Bloom's taxonomy of educational objectives* (Complete ed.). Longman.

Deci, E. L., Vallerand, R. J., Pelletier, L. G., & Ryan, R. M. (1991). Motivation and education: The self-determination perspective. *Educational Psychologist, 26*(3–4), 325–346. https://doi.org/10.1080/00461520.1991.9653137

Dunn, R., & Honigsfeld, A. (2013). Learning styles: what we know and what we need. *The Educational Forum, 77*(2), 225–232. https://doi.org/10.1080/00131725.2013.765328

Flowerday, T., & Schraw, G. (2003). Effect of choice on cognitive and affective engagement. *The Journal of Educational Research, 96*(4), 207–215. https://doi.org/10.1080/00220670309598810

Keen, D. (2001). *Talent in the new millennium. Research study, 2001–2002, into gifted education in the Bay of Plenty, Otago and Southland regions of New Zealand. Report on year 1 of the program* [Paper presentation]. The Australian Association for Research in Education, Perth, Australia.

Komarraju, M., Karau, S. J., Schmeck, R. R., & Avdic, A. (2011). The Big Five personality traits, learning styles, and academic achievement.

Personality and Individual Differences, 51(4), 472–477. https://doi.org/10.1016/j.paid.2011.04.019

Litman, J., Hutchins, T., & Russon, R. (2005). Epistemic curiosity, feeling-of-knowing, and exploratory behaviour. *Cognition and Emotion, 19*(4), 559–582. https://doi.org/10.1080/02699930441000427

Magner, L. (2000). Reaching all children through differentiated assessment: The 2-5-8 plan. *Gifted Child Today, 23*(3), 48–50. https://doi.org/10.1177/107621750002300313

Patall, E. A. (2013). Constructing motivation through choice, interest, and interestingness. *Journal of Educational Psychology, 105*(2), 522–534. https://doi.org/10.1037/a0030307

Ricca, J. (1984). Learning styles and preferred instructional strategies of gifted students. *Gifted Child Quarterly, 28*(3), 121–126. https://doi.org/10.1177/001698628402800305

Robinson, J., Patall, E. A., & Cooper, H. (2008). The effects of choice on intrinsic motivation and related outcomes: A meta-analysis of research findings. *Psychological Bulletin, 134*(2), 270–300. https://doi.org/10.1037/0033-2909.134.2.270

Sagan, L. L. (2010). Students' choice: Recommendations for environmental and instructional changes in school. *The Clearing House: A Journal of Educational Strategies, Issues and Ideas, 83*(6), 217–222. https://doi.org/10.1080/00098650903505407

Snyder, R. F. (1999). The relationship between learning styles/multiple intelligences and academic achievement of high school students. *The High School Journal, 83*(2), 11–20.

About the Author

After teaching science for more than 15 years, both overseas and in the U.S., **Laurie E. Westphal, Ed.D.,** now works as an independent gifted education and science consultant nationwide. She enjoys developing and presenting staff development on low-stress differentiation strategies and using menus for various districts and conferences, working with teachers to assist them in planning and developing lessons to meet the needs of their advanced students. Laurie currently resides in Houston, TX, and has made it her goal to convert as many teachers as she can to the differentiated lifestyle in the classroom and to share her vision for real-world, product-based lessons that help all students become critical thinkers and effective problem solvers. She is the author of the Differentiating Instruction With Menus series as well as *Hands-On Physical Science* and *Stress-Free Science*.

Common Core Standards and Next Generation Science Standards

This book aligns with an extensive number of the Common Core State Standards and Next Generation Science Standards. Please visit https://www.prufrock.com/ccss.aspx to download a complete packet of the standards that align with each individual menu in this book.